'Geoff Whitty has been a "must read" for all those in
role of education in achieving it for over 35 years. V
school leader or academic, you read, think and lear
generation it's like finding a glittering jewel of insig
brings his thinking into a coherent whole, and

Professor Sir Tim Brighouse, Norham Fellow, University of Oxford, and formerly Commissioner for London Schools

'In *Research and Policy in Education*, Geoff Whitty again demonstrates why he is among the most insightful analysts of education policy and of its assumptions and politics. And once again he shows that it is possible to write about these things in clear and compelling ways. This book is a fine addition to his many other contributions.'

Michael W. Apple, John Bascom Professor of Curriculum and Instruction and Educational Policy Studies, University of Wisconsin, Madison

'This is a timely and hugely significant book. As educational policymaking comes under increasing scrutiny, this book will serve as the benchmark for its analysis. Geoff Whitty brings all his experience as a leading policy analyst and policy adviser to bear with telling effect. The analysis of particular cases of policymaking is enlightening, critical and at the same time balanced. In this, his achievement is augmented by the team that have contributed to the book. This will be mandatory reading for anyone in the area.'

Hugh Lauder, Professor of Education and Political Economy, University of Bath

Research and Policy in Education

The Bedford Way Papers Series

28 *The Dearing Report: Ten years on*
   Edited by David Watson and Michael Amoah
29 *History, Politics and Policy-making in Education: A Festschrift presented to Richard Aldrich*
   Edited by David Crook and Gary McCulloch
30 *Public Sector Reform: Principles for improving the education system*
   Frank Coffield, Richard Steer, Rebecca Allen, Anna Vignoles, Gemma Moss and Carol Vincent
31 *Educational Resource Management: An international perspective*
   Derek Glover and Rosalind Levačić
32 *Education in a Global City: Essays from London*
   Edited by Tim Brighouse and Leisha Fullick
33 *Exploring Professionalism*
   Edited by Bryan Cunningham
34 *Music Education in the 21st Century in the United Kingdom: Achievements, analysis and aspirations*
   Edited by Susan Hallam and Andrea Creech
35 *Critical Practice in Teacher Education: A study of professional learning*
   Edited by Ruth Heilbronn and John Yandell
36 *Accelerated Leadership Development: Fast tracking school leaders*
   Peter Earley and Jeff Jones
37 *Post-Compulsory Education and Lifelong Learning across the United Kingdom: Policy, organisation and governance*
   Edited by Ann Hodgson, Ken Spours and Martyn Waring
38 *From Exam Factories to Communities of Discovery: The democratic route*
   Frank Coffield and Bill Williamson
39 *An Aims-based Curriculum: The significance of human flourishing for schools*
   Michael Reiss and John White
40 *Law, Education, Politics, Fairness: England's extreme legislation for education reform*
   Dan Gibton
41 *Making Evidence Matter: A new perspective for evidence-informed policy making in education*
   Chris Brown
42 *Browne and Beyond: Modernizing English higher education*
   Edited by Claire Callender and Peter Scott
43 *The Question of Conscience: Higher education and personal responsibility*
   Sir David Watson
44 *Professional Life in Modern British Higher Education*
   Edited by Bryan Cunningham
45 *Who Needs Examinations? A story of climbing ladders and dodging snakes*
   John White

A full list of Bedford Way Papers, including earlier books in the series, can be requested by emailing ioepress@ioe.ac.uk

Research and Policy in Education
Evidence, ideology and impact

Geoff Whitty
with Jake Anders, Annette Hayton, Sarah Tang and Emma Wisby

First published in 2016 by the UCL Institute of Education Press, University College London, 20 Bedford Way, London WC1H 0AL

ioepress.co.uk

© Geoff Whitty 2016

British Library Cataloguing in Publication Data:
A catalogue record for this publication is available from the British Library

ISBNs
978-1-78277-084-8 (paperback)
978-1-78277-142-5 (PDF eBook)
978-1-78277-143-2 (ePub eBook)
978-1-78277-144-9 (Kindle eBook)

All rights reserved. No part of this publication may be reproduced, stored in a retrieval system, or transmitted in any form or by any means, electronic, mechanical, photocopying, recording or otherwise, without the prior permission of the copyright owner.

Every effort has been made to trace copyright holders and to obtain their permission for the use of copyright material. The publisher apologizes for any errors or omissions and would be grateful if notified of any corrections that should be incorporated in future reprints or editions of this book.

The opinions expressed in this publication are those of the authors and do not necessarily reflect the views of any part of University College London.

Typeset by Quadrant Infotech (India) Pvt Ltd
Printed by CPI Group (UK) Ltd, Croydon CR0 4YY

Contents

Acknowledgements viii

About the authors ix

Introduction xi

1 Education(al) research and education policy in an imperfect world 1
 with Emma Wisby

2 Ideology and evidence in English teacher education 20

3 The (mis)use of evidence in policy borrowing: A transatlantic case study 38

4 'Closing the achievement gap': Rhetoric or reality? 55
 with Jake Anders

5 'Knowing the ropes'? Access to higher education in England 74
 with Annette Hayton and Sarah Tang

6 The continuing importance of the sociology of education 97

References 109

Index 131

Acknowledgements

All of the chapters of this book have been developed from earlier articles published over the past decade, as follows:

Chapter 1: Whitty, G. (2006) 'Education(al) research and education policy making: Is conflict inevitable?' *British Educational Research Journal*, 32 (2), 159–76. Published with permission from John Wiley and Sons.

Chapter 2: Whitty, G. (2014) 'Recent developments in teacher training and their consequences for the "University Project" in education'. *Oxford Review of Education*, 40 (4), 466–81. Published with permission from Taylor & Francis.

Chapter 3: Whitty, G. (2012) 'Policy tourism and policy borrowing in education: A Trans-Atlantic case study'. In Steiner-Khamsi, G. and F. Waldow, F. (eds), *World Yearbook of Education 2012: Policy borrowing and lending in education*. London: Routledge, 354–70. Published with permission from Taylor & Francis.

Chapter 4: Whitty, G. and Anders, J. (2014) 'Narrowing the achievement gap: Policy and practice in England 1997–2010'. In Clark, J.V. (ed.), *Closing the Achievement Gap from an International Perspective: Transforming STEM for effective education*. Dordrecht: Springer, 163–91. Published with permission from Springer.

Chapter 5: Whitty, G., Hayton, A. and Tang, S. (2015) 'Who you know, what you know and knowing the ropes: A review of evidence about access to higher education institutions in England'. *Review of Education*, 3 (1), 27–67. Published with permission from John Wiley and Sons.

Chapter 6: Whitty, G. (2012) 'A life with the sociology of education'. *British Journal of Educational Studies*, 60 (1), 65–75. Published with permission from Taylor & Francis.

About the authors

Geoff Whitty taught in primary and secondary schools before working at Bath University, the University of Wisconsin-Madison, King's College London, Bristol Polytechnic and Goldsmiths College. He joined the Institute of Education, University of London, as the Karl Mannheim Professor of Sociology of Education in 1992 and served as its Director between 2000 and 2010. He is now the Institute's Director Emeritus and holds a Global Innovation Chair in Equity in Higher Education at the University of Newcastle, Australia, as well as a Research Professorship in Education at Bath Spa University, UK. He is also a Visiting Professor at the Universities of Bath, Bedfordshire and Birmingham and an Honorary Research Fellow at the University of Oxford. He is a past President of the British Educational Research Association and of the College of Teachers. In 2011 he was awarded a CBE for services to teacher education.

Jake Anders is a Research Fellow at the National Institute of Economic and Social Research. He studied Philosophy, Politics and Economics at New College, University of Oxford and then completed a PhD in Economics of Education, focusing on socioeconomic inequality in access to higher education in England, at the UCL Institute of Education. Jake has also worked as a Committee Specialist at the House of Commons Education Committee. Jake's research seeks to understand the causes and consequences of inequality in education, and to evaluate policies and programmes aiming to reduce it.

Annette Hayton is Head of Widening Participation at the University of Bath and has many years of experience in managing activities designed to support successful progression to higher education, as well as in developing strategies to ensure that all students have a positive experience of university study. She is currently convenor of the UALL (Universities Association for Lifelong Learning) Widening Participation and Access Network; convenor of NERUPI (Network for Evaluating and Researching University Participation Interventions); member of ICHEM (International Centre for Higher Education Management) at the University of Bath; Chair of the Western Vocational Progression Consortium and the UNet Universities Network; and a member of the editorial board of *Widening Participation and Lifelong Learning*. Annette is interested in how educational theory can be developed and applied in practice to promote positive change within the education system, aiming to combine theory and practice in her work.

Sarah Tang is a Research Associate at Education Datalab and is studying towards a PhD from the UCL Institute of Education. Prior to this she worked as Evaluation Officer at the Education Endowment Foundation and as a Research Officer at UCL Institute of Education. She qualified as a Mathematics teacher as part of the inaugural Teach First cohort and her research interests include teacher quality and closing the attainment gap.

Emma Wisby is Head of Policy and Public Affairs at the UCL Institute of Education. Prior to that she was Committee Specialist to the then House of Commons Children, Schools and Families Select Committee, and a researcher in the field of education policy. She also undertook a review of school councils and pupil voice for the then Department for Education and Skills. Following her PhD at the University of Sheffield, which examined the post-Dearing shift to standards-based quality assurance in the UK higher education sector, she spent her early career conducting consultancy research for the education department and its various agencies.

Introduction

In a sense, this book is the third volume in a trilogy. In 1985, I published *Sociology and School Knowledge* (Methuen, 1985). This brought together and reflected upon the work I had been doing over the previous 15 years on how sociology could help us understand curriculum issues and struggles over the nature of schooling. In 2002, I brought together my work of the next 15 years in a book called *Making Sense of Education Policy* (Sage, 2002), which again used sociological perspectives to explore the provenance and impact of education policy in the UK and beyond. This third volume, *Research and Policy in Education*, gathers together some of the work I have undertaken in the past 15 years, for 10 of which I was Director of the Institute of Education, University of London (now UCL Institute of Education; IOE).[1]

When I became Director of the IOE in 2000, I relinquished the Karl Mannheim Chair in Sociology of Education and it will be evident that much of this book is less self-consciously sociological in its approach than the two earlier ones, engaging rather with generic issues in education research and education policy of the sort I encountered as Director. Yet it will also become clear that, as the book progresses, I become increasingly drawn back into using sociological perspectives to make sense of the phenomena I am discussing. Then, in the final chapter, I explicitly reaffirm my roots in the sociological tradition (though not necessarily contemporary approaches to the discipline) and reassert its importance for understanding and confronting some of the education policy dilemmas of today.

The book begins by exploring the extent to which research evidence on contemporary policy and practice in education is actually used in education policymaking and indeed how far it can even be expected to be. Despite claims by politicians of all parties that they engage in evidence-based policymaking, there is relatively little use of evidence, other than anecdotal, in their speeches and highly selective use of research evidence in government White Papers and the like. Not that education policy is alone in its failure to conform to the idealized tenets of evidence-informed policymaking, of course. As a member of the House of Commons Public Administration Select Committee once put it, 'much of our policy making is evidence free, prejudice driven and hysteria driven (particularly hysteria generated by the press)' (2009: Q 138).

While the first chapter discusses this and related issues in general terms, the next two chapters are case studies of just how far education policy sometimes strays from its evidence-based or evidence-informed rhetoric. One illustrates this in relation to the reform of teacher training in England under the Coalition Government, where policy seems to have been driven largely by New Right ideology rather than research evidence on the effectiveness of provision. The following chapter shows how the use of evidence in international policy borrowing falls far short of the protocols expected in academic research. It suggests that the rhetoric of 'what works' masks a predilection for reforms that are ideologically consistent with a wider agenda associated with what Sahlberg (2015) has termed the Global Educational Reform Movement.[2]

The next two chapters fulfil a commitment I made when I retired as Director of the IOE at the end of 2010 that one of the projects I would undertake would be to review the research evidence on ways of narrowing the social class achievement and participation gap. Both narrowing the socio-economic 'achievement gap' in schools and the push to 'widen participation' in higher education have been policies driven largely by political and economic imperatives. Neither policy has been systematically evaluated, which is hardly surprising when the Organisation for Economic Co-operation and Development (OECD) (2015) tells us that 90 per cent of education reforms are not properly evaluated. So these two chapters accept that governments have not lived up to their own ideals of evidence-informed policymaking, and that we therefore have to adopt a pragmatic approach to evidence. Yet in both cases there is credible research and evaluation evidence on aspects of the policies that can be drawn upon to help understand their limits and possibilities.

However, even in this context, the evidence does not simply speak for itself and, in writing these chapters, I found myself drawing upon sociological theories, especially theories of social and cultural reproduction, to help make sense of the policies and their impact. Hence, as indicated earlier, I end the book with a plea for discipline-based research on education, and here specifically the sociology of education, to remain part of that broad-based conception of the field of education research advocated in Chapter 1.

Much of my research in education has been collaborative and the work included in this book is no exception. Three of the chapters are explicitly co-authored – with Jake Anders, Annette Hayton, Sarah Tang and Emma Wisby – but my collaborators should not be held responsible for the broader context in which I have now located our collective work. I am also indebted to large numbers of colleagues and friends who have commented on drafts and helped me think through ideas. Again, they should not feel responsible for the way those ideas have come out in this book.

Notes

[1] This book is primarily about education research and policy in England, albeit with occasional cross-references to parallel developments elsewhere. This is somewhat ironic as much of my work, especially in the past five years or so, has been in and about Australia, the USA and China. See, for example, Whitty and Clement (2015) and Yan and Whitty (in press).

[2] It has been suggested to me that this book is about English education under 'neo-liberalism'. It may well be but I have chosen to use that term sparingly here. In too much contemporary writing on education, including some of my own, it is used to explain everything and ends up explaining little, if anything. In this book, I have preferred to restrict its use, like that of neo-conservatism, to refer to a particular strand of New Right thinking. For a nuanced discussion of 'neo-liberalism' in contemporary policy, see Gerrard (2015).

Chapter 1

Education(al) research and education policy in an imperfect world
with Emma Wisby

Introduction

In 2005 we drafted what would be the British Educational Research Association (BERA) presidential address for that year, which was subsequently published in the *British Educational Research Journal* (Whitty, 2006). In it we focused on what was becoming a key issue for education research at the time in England – the 'what works' agenda and the push from government for research to be oriented ever more strongly towards offering immediate answers to questions of policy and practice. In this chapter we revisit that paper and reflect on subsequent developments. We discuss how the related (and inter-related) notions of 'evidence-based' policy and practice and 'research for use' have been pursued with increasing enthusiasm, but without resolution of some difficult issues.

One of our prime concerns in 2005 was the possible narrowing of the kinds of education research deemed worthy of funding.[1] We argued that, while we should expect some education research to be aligned in various ways with immediate questions of policy, some of it would be regarded by governments, rightly or wrongly, as being of limited value, despite its importance to the development of education as a field of study. Theoretical work in the foundation disciplines, for example, might fall into this category. Some of the 'policy-facing' research, we added, might not be supportive of current reform agendas and might well be seen as oppositional to government policy. However, we felt that such a range of orientations was entirely appropriate for education research in a free society. We remain of the view that a healthy education research community must be a broad church, encompassing activity that responds directly to external priorities, but also curiosity- or discipline-led inquiry.

So far, schools of education in English universities have adapted to the growing culture of research for use without abandoning their wider research mission. There have, however, been a number of new warnings that this breadth is under threat and that both 'blue skies' and 'critical' research traditions are, in particular, precariously positioned. A more instrumental approach on the part of government to funding education research, as well as the new 'impact agenda' in research policy more generally, could each require schools of education to think very differently about how they sustain, and therefore shape, their research activity in future (e.g. BERA–UCET, 2012). The same changes might also influence the decisions that individual researchers make about the direction of their work. Parallel shifts in initial teacher education (ITE) policy towards a 'schools-led' system, as discussed in Chapter 2 of this book, are compounding these pressures on schools of education and their research.

In the present chapter we discuss these continuing challenges to the diversity of the field, but we want also to focus on some difficult issues that arise for those who believe that education research should be undertaken largely if not exclusively with a view to informing policy and practice. This is a sentiment that is found among researchers as well as policymakers (e.g. Black and Wiliam, 2003). It is not clear, however, that it is understood in the same way by all parties.

It is important not to gloss over the disjunctions that exist between policy-facing research and the realities of policymaking in practice. We highlighted in the earlier paper just how far research and policymaking would need to travel in order to live up to the apparent goals of evidence-based policymaking, even if this was based on a shared understanding and unanimously recognized as a desirable development. Thus, there is a danger that, if the research-for-use agenda becomes the main driver in research policy and funding, education research might not only become narrower, but might operate on a false prospectus – leading to frustration on all sides, as well as a denuded discipline and, ultimately, less considered policymaking and practice.

This chapter therefore explores the possibilities and limits of the turn towards education research being conceived primarily as the handmaiden of policy and practice.[2] Before that, however, we need to introduce the problem of definitions. So far in this paper we have ourselves employed a number of terms to characterize the favoured relationship between research and policy, settling on 'research for use' as a shorthand. This reflects the wider debate, where many different terms are used interchangeably and without precision. It is this absence of clear definitions and goals that has often allowed underlying complexities (and differences of view) to remain unexplored behind terms employed as rhetorical slogans.

The issue is not so much whether there should be constructive engagement between research and user communities, but rather how far it should go, and what form it should take. With regard to the former issue, the uncertainties are illustrated in the growing sense among researchers that they prefer the term 'research-informed' (or 'evidence-informed'), rather than 'research-based' or 'research-led' policy (Pollard, 2015), a version that arguably would also afford policymakers more 'wriggle room'. Bennett (2015) has offered 'research-augmented' as a term more accurately reflecting the potential (or limits) of research use, in this case by teachers. Indeed, the recent interchange between Wiliam (2015), Bennett (2015), and Collins (2015) suggests that the rhetoric around teaching as a research-led profession is as problematic as the language of research-led policy.

Then there are differing assumptions about the types of research that are (most) relevant to policy or practice. Over 40 years ago, in his inaugural address to the newly formed BERA, John Nisbet claimed that we had moved away from 'the naïve idea that problems are solved by educational research' or what he called the 'old educational science idea' (Nisbet, 1974). Rather, he characterized the relationship between research and policy as 'indirect' and more about 'sensitizing' policymakers to problems than solving them. Yet the current 'what works' agenda has seen a resurgence of the educational science idea, not least in the enthusiasm of many policymakers (and some researchers) for a medical model of educational research in which experimental methods, and particularly randomized control trials (RCTs), are regarded as the 'gold standard' (see Jadad and Enkin, 2007). Systematic reviews come a close second (see Gough *et al.*, 2012). It may be that Nisbet's warning that educational research may not provide 'final answers to questions, or objective evidence to settle controversies', and his support for a 'spectrum' of types of research, need to be heeded afresh. We return to these arguments at the end of the chapter after reviewing the recent history of the surrounding debate.

Education research under New Labour and the Coalition

Debate between the education research community and governments on the nature and value of research outputs is nothing new. Nisbet (1974) himself reported remarks made by Margaret Thatcher, while Secretary of State for Education and Science, expressing frustration that too much research sponsored by her department was not relevant to its needs or its timetable. In her own BERA presidential address 20 years later, Jean Rudduck (1994) cited a number of such examples from those first two decades of the association's existence. Nevertheless, by the 1990s these matters had come to the fore, with a succession of commentators questioning the value of much of the work that constituted education research.

Reviews of the quality, funding and use of research in education were undertaken for the Economic and Social Research Council (ESRC) (the research council most involved in supporting education research) in 1991 and 1995, and just a few years later for the Leverhulme Trust (see Rudduck and McIntyre, 1998). But the debate soon became dominated by a series of seemingly damning (although sometimes contradictory) reports for the then Teacher Training Agency (TTA) (Hargreaves, 1996), Office for Standards in Education (Ofsted) (Tooley and Darby, 1998) and the Department for Education and Employment (DfEE) itself (Hillage *et al.*, 1998). Although the overall picture was not entirely bleak, those reading the headlines and press reports could perhaps have been forgiven for believing that UK educational research as a whole was defined by a series of failings: a lack of rigour, an absence of cumulative research findings, theoretical incoherence, ideological bias, irrelevance to schools, lack of involvement of teachers, inaccessibility and poor dissemination – together resulting in poor cost-effectiveness. All education research was in danger of being tarred with the same brush and judged as wanting, certainly as a contributor to policy and practice. This was by no means a purely UK phenomenon: for example, the education research community in the USA has faced similar scrutiny of the quality, relevance and impact of its work (e.g. Center for Education, 2004), as have Australian researchers (see Yates, 2005). Our focus here, however, is the relationship between education research and policymaking in England since 1997.

This issue had by this time become particularly high profile because the New Labour Government that came to power in Britain in 1997 had proclaimed its commitment to evidence-based policy and an emphasis on finding out and disseminating 'what works' – not least for its top priority of 'education, education, education' (Blair, 1996). It was New Labour's founding commitment to the 'Third Way' that brought with it the mantra of 'what works'. Influential in the US since the 1980s, it was adopted enthusiastically by New Labour as part of Tony Blair's modernization of the Labour Party. Although the election of New Labour in May 1997 did not bring in a golden age for educational research, there were some important and positive contrasts with what had gone before. In rhetorical terms at least, an emphasis on the value of research evidence provided a welcome change. And, as Furlong (2005) pointed out, it also brought resources: in the party's first three years in government, annual research expenditure in the English education department almost doubled from £5.4 million to over £10.4 million. In 2011/12, the last year significantly influenced by Labour Government spending commitments, expenditure on research and evaluation had reached £12.1 million (Brown, 2014). From 1997 this expenditure supported several major research programmes and centres that were based at universities in England, such as the Centre for the Economics of Education and the Centre for Research on the Wider Benefits of Learning. The major budgets associated with some of the key government programmes funded significant research operations, including, for example, the National Research and Development Centre for Adult Literacy and Numeracy.

The department and its equivalents in the devolved administrations, together with the Higher Education Funding Council for England (HEFCE) and others, were also involved in the ESRC-managed Teaching and Learning Research Programme, which was the largest programme of research in education in UK history. This £30 million programme, which ran from 2000 to 2011, was specifically designed to fund research with the potential to improve outcomes for learners and, to that end, to promote the application of its findings.

Alongside this, there was an attempt to bring greater coherence to educational research, in terms of both synthesizing research that was already available and coordinating future projects. From 2000, the department funded a programme of systematic reviews of educational research, supported by the Evidence for Policy and Practice Information and Coordinating Centre (EPPI Centre) (see Oakley, 2002).

A National Educational Research Forum (NERF) was set up in 1999 with the aim of better coordinating research efforts. Aspirations for something similar had existed since at least the early 1970s, and a more low-key Schools Research Liaison Group had pre-dated NERF as a mechanism by which the department and non-departmental public bodies shared research agendas. NERF, though, sought an altogether higher profile as well as a strategic role in the future of educational research.

However, greater public visibility and funding under New Labour were not without their costs for educational research, let alone education research as a whole. This manifested itself in a growing attitude of 'who pays the piper calls the tune', aligned with a fairly narrow and mechanistic understanding of research relevance.

Early in Tony Blair's government, David Blunkett, Secretary of State for Education and Employment from 1997 to 2001, looked at the research–policy relationship in a 2000 ESRC lecture entitled 'Influence or irrelevance?' (Blunkett, 2000). While he acknowledged that there were faults on both 'sides', he nevertheless threw down the gauntlet to the social science community as a whole to contribute more directly and 'productively' to policymaking. Some academics read his lecture as a demand that their research should support government policy (e.g. Hodgkinson, 2000). After all, on taking office, he had told head teachers that the 'cynics' and 'energy sappers' should move aside rather than 'erode the enthusiasm and hope that currently exists' (Gardiner, 1997). One of his ministerial colleagues, Charles Clarke, was wont to complain that educational research in particular never gave him anything useful, and throughout his time as a junior minister and later as Secretary of State there were rumours that he wanted to do something drastic about educational research. The setting-up of a series of 'development and research centres' focused on improving standards in education was mooted, though it never actually materialized.

These attitudes – reminiscent of what Nisbet (1974) regarded as an outdated 'educational science' style of research, and what Gewirtz (2003) more recently characterized as the 'hyper-rationalist-technicist' approach – were evident across a range of government agencies. For Gewirtz, this approach was epitomized by David Hargreaves's call, on behalf of the TTA, for research that:

> (i) demonstrates conclusively that if teachers change their practice from x to y there will be a significant and enduring improvement in teaching and learning and (ii) has developed an effective method of convincing teachers of the benefits of, and means to, changing from x to y.
>
> (Hargreaves, 1996: 5)

Hargreaves's position was arguably more sophisticated than Gewirtz's interpretation, but something close was certainly implicit in a draft of the first consultation paper produced by NERF (2000), which seemed to advocate a particularly limited and instrumental view of research. The view of one education researcher who saw the draft was that it treated research as 'about providing accounts of what works for unselfconscious classroom drones to implement' and that it portended 'an absolute standardisation of research purposes, procedures, reporting and dissemination' (Ball, 2001: 266–7). Similar criticisms were levelled at the emphasis on systematic reviewing (e.g. MacLure, 2005). The NERF consultation exercise actually led to the acknowledgement of the need for a pluralist view of research, but it also continued to argue for a means of prioritizing resources based on research making a 'worthwhile contribution' to education and 'maximising impact' (NERF, 2001).

Although NERF itself was disbanded in 2006, government enthusiasm for the rhetoric of evidence-based policy in education continued throughout the New Labour era and on into the next government, the Conservative–Liberal Democrat Coalition that was in power from 2010 to 2015. The orientation shifted a little in terms of presentation: in particular, developments at the Department for Education (DfE) from 2010 onwards reflected the Coalition's wider emphasis on raising standards through the further devolution of decision-making to schools, in place of New Labour's early penchant for national initiatives and strategies. Nevertheless, evidence-based policy remained an important feature.

By now, due at least in part to economic austerity, government spending on (education) research had reduced dramatically. Against this backdrop, one of the Coalition's early moves was to provide seed funding for an Education Endowment Foundation (EEF), a grant-making charity 'dedicated to challenging educational disadvantage in English primary and secondary schools' by sharing evidence on effective practice.[3] One of the ways in which the EEF has sought to achieve this is through its Learning and Teaching Toolkit. The toolkit synthesizes the findings from systematic reviews and trials into an online facility, allowing the user to compare the estimated impact and cost of different types of educational intervention. It already encompasses over 10,000 pieces of research, and remains a 'live' resource that is regularly updated (EEF, 2012).[4] The EEF also commissions research, in which it is largely committed to funding and evaluating RCT-type studies. In a sense, this initiative is very explicitly about generating more quantitative research in education (see Collins, 2015). To this extent, it is a welcome antidote to the emphasis on purely qualitative methods in much education research in recent decades and builds on the passionate case made for the employment of quantitative methods, including RCTs, by our colleague Ann Oakley (2000).

In the same vein, in 2013, the education department published *Building Evidence into Education*, a paper by science commentator Ben Goldacre, which further argued the case for greater use of trials to inform education policymaking and classroom practice (Goldacre, 2013). This reflected Goldacre's own background in medicine, where this approach has revolutionized practice, albeit that such a culture took at least 50 years to establish itself among doctors and debate continues within the profession as to the appropriateness of a narrowly trials-led approach. While the government may have been disappointed with the apparent lack of momentum behind the report subsequent to its publication, the exercise has served as a further 'nudge' towards a more direct and explicit relationship between research, policy and practice in education research funding.

Developments in higher education research policy, many of them set in train under New Labour but developed under the Coalition, have reinforced these shifts, again partly reflecting the pressures of economic austerity. Of central importance here are the research councils and research funding distributed through the higher education funding councils, given that these are the main sources of funding for basic research and researcher-led inquiry.

Although the ESRC itself remains committed to funding a broad spectrum of types of research, it now devotes an increasing proportion of its budget to designated 'priorities', leaving less 'responsive-mode' funding for what are essentially open calls for proposals from the research community. Alongside this, and in collaboration with the other research councils, government and third-sector partners, the ESRC has invested in a series of 'what works centres' focused on research synthesis and RCTs. These centres include the EEF and, among others, centres on early intervention, local economic growth and crime reduction (see, for example, What Works Network, 2014). In addition, the ESRC has forged a number of co-funded research calls with government departments.

More generally, in 2009 Research Councils UK (RCUK), the umbrella organization for all the research councils, implemented 'Pathways to Impact', which introduced consideration of potential economic and societal impact as a mandatory part of research grant applications (see RCUK, 2015).[5] This encompasses conceptual impact (shifting understanding of policy and practice, reframing debates) and capacity-building impact (supporting technical and personal skills development) as well as instrumental impact on policy and practice (shaping legislation, altering behaviour) (see Nutley *et al.*, 2007). It represents a new feature in the process of applying for research council funding: all grant applicants now have to complete an 'impact summary' and a longer Pathways to Impact statement identifying potential for economic and societal impact, which is treated separately from academic impact. This is about embedding knowledge exchange and research impact in all research-council-funded projects. Impact Acceleration Accounts (IAAs) have been added to take this beyond individual projects and support culture change at institutional level (the ESRC has to date allocated IAA funding to 24 institutions). Larger research-council-funded centres can access 'Impact Uplift' funding to take advantage of impact-related opportunities that arise. A linked development has been the emergence of national initiatives on public engagement in research, which are seen as furthering research impact. The National Coordinating Centre for Public Engagement (NCCPE) was established in 2008, funded by the four UK higher education funding councils, RCUK, and the Wellcome Trust. It published its manifesto for public engagement, to which universities are invited to sign up to demonstrate their commitment to involving external audiences in their research, from inception to design and dissemination.

A further driver in research policy comes from changes to the periodic national assessment of universities' research, which is conducted by HEFCE and used to allocate research funding on a block-grant basis. Through this process HEFCE currently invests around £315 million in social science each year, compared to the ESRC's circa £140 million.

Assessment of UK universities' research was first introduced in 1986 and a Research Assessment Exercise (RAE) was subsequently conducted approximately every five years. While often credited with the UK's strong international performance on citations, policy makers have also regarded this exercise as encouraging researchers to focus too much on producing academic publications for peer review. Partly in response to these concerns, for the 2014 assessment the RAE was replaced by the Research Excellence Framework (REF), under which the assessment of research impact (in addition to the traditional focus on the quality of research outputs and institutional research environment) got its first outing. Accounting for 20 per cent of a university's score, impact for REF purposes was defined as: "An effect on, change or benefit to the economy, society, culture, public policy or services, health, the environment or quality of life, beyond academia" (HEFCE, 2011a). In practice, this definition has been much narrower than that used by the research councils, being much more focused on instrumental impact. Universities were required to submit a statement on how they facilitate research impact, alongside case studies illustrating the impact of their research (essentially one case study for up to every 10 researchers returned for assessment). In the immediate aftermath of the REF, the inclusion of 'impact' has been deemed a success by both the government and HEFCE – and many in the higher education sector – and is very likely to remain part of research assessment, if not become a growing element of it.

Along with the structural and policy drivers outlined, a significant movement for evidence-informed policy and research for use has also emerged, particularly under the Coalition. A good example here is the work of the Alliance for Useful Evidence, established in 2012 by the ESRC, innovation charity Nesta and the Big Lottery Fund in order to 'champion the use of evidence in decision-making for social policy and practice' (see www.alliance4usefulevidence.org). It has published widely on research–policy links and how to further this cause. In education, the Alliance has also helped to establish the Education Media Centre, to encourage and support the media in making greater use of educational research in its reporting on education issues. Think tanks, learned societies and subject associations have all engaged in this debate (see, for example, Haddon *et al.*, 2015; Mulgan and Puttick, 2013; Nelson and O'Beirne, 2014; Nutley *et al.*, 2013; Puttick, 2011; Sharples, 2013).

Across disciplines and policy fields, the discussions as to what is impeding 'better' and more consistent use of research in policy typically identify the same issues of supply and demand. Communication is a central concern: jargon-heavy publications; the absence of concise summaries; the lack of infrastructure for research translation (beyond the medical sciences); and the lack of access to journal publications among policy audiences are all cited.[6] Incentives within academia that do not reward efforts directed at research impact are also often picked out (and here the REF is seen both as friend and foe).[7] On the demand side, politicians' poor grasp of science and statistics has been highlighted and remedies offered (G. Arnett, 2015); meanwhile, the 'fact-checking' movement, particularly evident in the run-up to the 2015 general election, has sought to engender more responsible use of data in policy debate and reporting (e.g. www.fullfact.org).

Responding to the critique of educational research

In the 2005 BERA address we made a brief assessment of the picture painted by the critical reviews of the 1990s and New Labour ministers' subsequent assertions that educational research as it stood was often of poor quality and largely irrelevant to the government's task in education. As we noted at the time, no one who regularly reviewed papers and research proposals could deny that there was some poor quality research in education, but then so there was in medicine and other fields with which education was often (and still is) unfavourably compared. This is despite the fact that, for many years, education was one of the social sciences that the ESRC regarded as meeting world-class quality criteria (Diamond, 2005). Even more recently, a government state-of-the-nation report on university research singled out education and used it as a case study of national excellence (BIS, 2011). In RAE terms, the discipline's grade profile in the 2001 exercise had been disappointing. But by the 2008 RAE it performed more strongly (Brown, 2009), and in the most recent assessment, the 2014 REF, the overall proportion of top grade (4*, 'world-leading') activity in education, at 30 per cent, was exactly the average for all units of assessment across the entire exercise. As Pollard (2015: 10) put it: 'Education has "held its own".'[8]

As regards the charge of irrelevance to the needs of government, there was always research that could usefully have informed policy, even on policymakers' own terms. Either this charge was to misrepresent education research, or part of a narrow push for research in the education science mould. Yet a field defined too narrowly would provide a very limited evidence base for improving an education system and informing a teaching profession facing the challenges of a rapidly changing world, where what works today may not work tomorrow. It is important and even useful, therefore, for educational research to be able to ask other sorts of questions as well as 'what works', if only *why* something works and why it works in some contexts and not in others. This is something that the US Institute of Education Sciences belatedly recognized by giving greater priority to putting research findings into context and asking 'how, why, for whom, and under what conditions' policies are effective (see

National Board for Educational Sciences, 2010). But, equally importantly for our purposes, it is also appropriate that policy debate should be informed by research that asks more fundamental questions and that questions prevailing assumptions, including about what a 'just' education involves (Gale and Densmore, 2003).

The challenge for the education research community remains the same as in 2005: to take the criticisms of its research seriously and redress genuine shortcomings and imbalances while also defending its breadth, such that others' assumptions and priorities do not come to reshape the field in their own image. This means resisting attempts to impose narrow or inappropriate quality criteria, themselves based in narrowly formulated notions of use and impact – and that, as we go on to discuss, are naïve about policymaking and/or the power of research therein. Back in 2005, the 'worst case scenario' was that research in the 'what works' mould became the only sort of research in education that was able to attract funding on any scale. The EEF represents a clear step in that direction, but constitutes just one funder of educational research. Wider shifts have been less decisive, but their longer-term effects might not be so different. The REF itself has seemed to imply a linear relationship between research outputs and research impact. One of the main findings of an evaluation of universities' REF preparations has been the difficulty that teams had in evidencing impact in this regard (Manville *et al.*, 2015: 16). While highly speculative at this stage, some respondents to the study voiced concerns that in the future universities and researchers would prioritize research that can more easily demonstrate impact (Manville *et al.*, 2015: 26). This is not about researchers slavishly orienting their work according to the REF requirements overnight, but subtle shifts in the overall profile of research.

On this point it is perhaps notable that the impact agenda is affecting how disciplines are presenting themselves to external audiences. In recent years there has been a series of reports defending the value of social science research, each of which has 'showcased' how research has contributed to policy agendas (e.g. Michie and Cooper, 2015; see also Bastow *et al.*, 2014). The most recent example is the 2015 Campaign for Social Science report *The Business of People*. As Holmwood (2015) observes, this report is largely focused on behavioural science and the use of big data, and how they can contribute to policy decisions – in short, research for the purpose of informing behavioural nudges within existing social structures. In the summer of 2013, BERA itself published a briefing paper along similar lines, entitled *Why Educational Research Matters*. This is based on a series of case studies of educational research to demonstrate 'the positive impact on policy and practice' (BERA, 2013). Both reports are targeted at politicians, to that end unashamedly instrumental in their orientation and, rightly or wrongly, do not seek to represent social science or education research in the round. This is not to suggest that disciplines should not influence policy and practice – indeed Chapter 6 of this book argues for the importance of sociology of education in that respect – but it would be unfortunate if it were to be seen as their only purpose.

We see related risks in the advocacy surrounding evidence-informed policy and research for use that has gained momentum in recent years. The contribution of advocacy organizations to bringing research, policy and practice closer together has been considerable. This has begun to remove the obvious barriers to dialogue across these communities, not least in relation to the presentation and packaging of research findings. This advocacy, however, has not typically engaged with the limitations of the research–policy relationship, other than to decry examples of 'policy-based evidence'. The focus is on achieving cultural change on both sides, and there is, understandably, no room for such a distraction. The result, however, is to perpetuate a lack of clarity as to what ultimately is being aimed for, let alone what can realistically be achieved in practice – at least without a fundamental overhaul of our political system.

We are not questioning the general aspiration to strengthen the interchange between research and policy. We are, however, highlighting how utopian visions of the relationship between research and policy could feed a particular climate around research policy and funding. Even a cursory look at how the relationship works 'on the ground' demonstrates the false prospectus that this vision would represent.

The realities of the use of research in policymaking

David Blunkett (2000) himself recognized the need for government to give more serious consideration to 'difficult' findings. But how realistic is this in practice? Even if research were of the highest quality and provided robust evidence on a given issue, would governments consistently seek it out and make good use of it so that it – above all else – was genuinely informing their decisions on policy? Various examples from the New Labour and Coalition administrations would suggest not, and few would suggest so unequivocally. In the process, these examples illustrate how in politics other factors will often take precedence over what the research evidence says. These include electioneering, the personal beliefs and commitments of politicians and their advisors, and, more simply, budgets, and the received wisdom of public opinion, and the constraints that these place on what can realistically be achieved in practice and how – matters of basic political expediency.[9]

The first example we cited in the BERA address was the use that New Labour made of evidence on class size during the 1997 general election. Evidence on the effects of class size is notoriously contentious and difficult to interpret, and the controversies continue to this day (e.g. Blatchford *et al.*, 2004; Blatchford, 2015). Even so, New Labour's commitment to cut class sizes at Key Stage 1 traded quite consciously on research findings accepted by most researchers and most teachers – evidence that if smaller classes have an unambiguously positive impact anywhere it is most marked in the very early years of schooling and in the most socially disadvantaged areas. So, the manifesto commitment to cut class sizes at Key Stage 1 to below 30 using monies that had formerly been used to send academically able children to private schools looked like a socially progressive policy based on robust research findings. As a policy, however, it was probably driven as much by the findings of election opinion polling as those of educational research: most classes over 30 were in marginal suburban constituencies, not in inner-city areas where classes were already below that level. Equally, some even more robust findings on the beneficial effects of cutting infant class size to 15 in disadvantaged areas did not influence the policy at all, presumably because it would have been extremely expensive, but possibly also because additional votes in these inner-city constituencies would not swing the election (Whitty, 2002).

The battle to gain power is one thing, and perhaps research evidence being used in this way under those circumstances is a case apart. Once in power, however, New Labour proceeded to make quite selective use of research evidence, and it was not always especially concerned about the quality of a research study if it served its policy purposes. The example we gave was the way in which research was used in the English White Paper of 2001, *Schools: Achieving success* (DfES, 2001). A central plank of the White Paper was to encourage secondary schools to specialize in certain areas of the curriculum in order to boost achievement. In making its case on 'specialist schools' the White Paper made much of research carried out for the then Technology Colleges Trust, which claimed to show that these schools added more value to their pupils' achievements than other schools. The problem was that the research had not been submitted to peer review and indeed was subsequently subject to public criticism by education statisticians. As one of those statisticians commented:

> It is not clear whether the authors of the White Paper sought views on the adequacy of the research before using it, but ... there are those within the DfES itself who would have cautioned against taking the results of the study at face value. Given that the research supported what was already Government policy, it would seem that this is what drove the decision to use it as 'evidence'.
>
> (Goldstein, 2001; see also Whitty, 2004)

Another example is provided by the academies programme. Here our concern is with the extent to which other drivers meant that the New Labour Government strayed from its avowed commitment to evidence-based policy. First of all, it largely disregarded a critical PricewaterhouseCoopers report (DfES, 2005a).[10] But serious questions were also raised about the way in which it used performance data to claim that these schools were, in general, performing better for equivalent pupils than the schools they had replaced and thereby justify continuing with the policy. After his own analysis of these data, Gorard (2005) commented:

> [A]ny improvement may take time and will be very challenging, and it would be hasty to condemn the programme as a whole on the [limited data available so far]. On the other hand, it is quite clear that it would be equally hasty and far less warranted to credit the programme with success at this stage. Yet this is what the government and the academies are doing. To point this out is not to make a criticism of the individuals involved or their practice, but of the way in which policy is being made on the basis of little useful evidence, and is seldom allowed to be seen to fail for electoral reasons. To expand the [academies] programme on the basis of what has happened so far is so removed from the evidence-based policy making that is a mantra of government today that it is scarcely worth pointing out.
>
> (Gorard, 2005: 376)

The House of Commons Education and Skills Select Committee (2005) similarly used both the specialist school and academies programmes to argue that, despite the government's proclaimed attachment to evidence-based policy, expensive schemes were being rolled out before having been adequately tested and evaluated compared to other less expensive alternatives (House of Commons Education and Skills Select Committee, 2005: 17). For a government keen to make its mark and quickly address serious shortcomings in the school system, this sense of urgency is understandable, but piloting and evaluation take time. Similar issues of policy running ahead of evidence have been raised in relation to the Coalition's extension of the academies programme (House of Commons Education Select Committee, 2015). Evidence about the effectiveness of this programme is discussed in Chapter 4.

There are other examples of the problematic use of data that have not been accounted for after the fact: take, for example, Peter Tymms's analysis of the 2005 National Curriculum Key Stage 2 performance data, which seemed to demonstrate that the government's much proclaimed success in raising standards in primary schools was no such thing (Mansell, 2005). Whether the original claim was simply down to a speechwriter without the requisite statistical training, we will never know, but if nothing else it reflects the pressures of political office and the need to demonstrate results. Other such examples can be found since 2010: on more than one occasion the Coalition administration used research data selectively to add weight to policy decisions in a way that at best exaggerated the actual message of the data and wider evidence base in question. Instances include Ofsted's misleading presentation of inspection data on school-based teacher training (Maddern, 2013), discussed further in Chapter 2, and the then Secretary of State Michael Gove's (and Ofsted's) less than robust use of international data to denigrate the performance of England's education system in comparison to that of other countries. Once analysis by John Jerrim demonstrated that the data showed no such pattern, it earned the DfE and Ofsted a rebuke by the UK Statistics Authority (UK Statistics Authority, 2012).

Where politicians have put their hands up to failings or less than expected progress, time could have been saved by paying greater attention to the existing research evidence. While New Labour ministers and their teams had engaged with the evidence on school improvement, they had not taken seriously the research on the limitations of taking a blanket approach to the roll-out of national initiatives. Prior to New Labour taking office, this research had suggested that if all schools were brought up to the level of the best as defined by school effectiveness research the social class gap in performance would be even starker than it was already – unless, that is, positive action was taken to provide extra targeted support for disadvantaged pupils (Mortimore and Whitty, 1997). Little surprise, then, that by 2005 data showed that the attainment gap between primary school children from disadvantaged and more advantaged backgrounds had not reduced (Kelly, 2005a). Thankfully, belated recognition of the problem did then lead to greater support for targeted interventions, such as Reading Recovery.

In the 2005 address we did identify some examples of the use of research by New Labour that on the face of it seemed more positive. A frequently cited example at the time was research on the importance of formative assessment and 'assessment for learning'. The synthesis of this research by colleagues based at King's College London (Black and Wiliam, 1998) had been particularly influential – for example, informing New Labour's Secondary National Strategy for a time. However, one interpretation is that this influence was achieved at least in part by demonstrating that formative assessment could raise attainment according to official indicators (Gewirtz, 2003). Given the tension between the summative assessment demanded by contemporary school performance indicators and the aspiration to support deeper learning that sits behind formative assessment, this is a matter of concern. But it reminds us again of the complexity of policymaking.

Against this background, the example of research influencing policy that still stands out the most, 10 years on from the BERA address, cited often by New Labour and the Coalition alike, is the EPPSE (formerly EPPE) project. The significance of this large-scale, longitudinal study of the effectiveness of different forms of early years provision was evident in Ruth Kelly's first major speech as Secretary of State for Education, when she said:

> There is considerable evidence … that sustained investment in early years support and education works. The most important ongoing study is probably the Effective Provision of Pre-school Education (EPPE) study. This exciting new evidence means we can now say definitively … that high quality pre-school experiences have lasting effects and continue to make a real difference to how well children do and how they develop soundly throughout the early years of primary school. This is especially so for those children from disadvantaged backgrounds.
>
> (Kelly, 2005b)

In England alone this research has been associated with a significant and sustained shift in investment to the early years, and has been cited in reforms to policy and spending, curriculum design, service delivery and professional practice. As some of this evidence had been around for some time, we conceded that this case could equally be regarded as simply another example of research being ignored until it suited the government. But the fact that this study achieved the profile it did in policy debates – and has continued to do so – is of note. What this example particularly demonstrates is that whether research is used constructively in policy debates or not (whatever the other contributing forces) depends on the research, and on researchers as well as politicians. One of the directors of the EPPSE project summarized it thus:

> [I]t is possible to influence government policy at national and local level through a combination of rigorous research methods, user-friendly dissemination, the combining of quantitative and qualitative approaches, and adequately funded research activity.
>
> (Sylva, 2004: 1)

The scale of the study's profile is testament to the team's approach throughout – engaging closely and responsively with policymakers, practitioners, early years providers and schools as well as parent groups. That is why the study is often held up as an exemplar of what can be achieved through social research connected to policy concerns, and these researchers have worked extensively with the research community – including through the advocacy organizations we noted earlier – to share their experience. The EPPSE project might have been regarded as 'pushing against an open door' in impact terms but, even in that context, the team made their own luck.

Implications for the future

Our concern in 2005, as now, was not to produce a balance sheet of pluses and minuses in policymakers' use of evidence, but to draw out the complexities of the research–policy relationship and consider the implications for the education research community.

As we have seen, much has changed over the past decade. Many organizations – and indeed many researchers – are advocating greater use of research evidence in policymaking and more research designed explicitly for use. Linked to this, there has been more active engagement from the research community in policy and impact agendas. Changes to funding levers, not least the REF, have supported this shift. Pollard (2015: 11) sees ('optimistically', as he puts it) a 'revitalised impetus towards evidence-informed policy and practice' stemming from the REF and its demonstration of the quality and relevance of education research. He suggests this could 'further promote *demand* for the knowledge and skills generated by education research' (11; emphasis in original), but underlines that it is the responsibility of every stakeholder – researchers, practitioners, civil servants, regulators, policymakers and others – to make the best use of that knowledge and expertise.

Research can influence policy (and practice) in different ways, but this will often be indirect and sometimes in ways that were not intended – as Nisbet (1974) pointed out all those years ago (see also Calhoun, 2014). Thus, research is best understood as a means of helping policymakers reconsider issues, think differently, reconceptualize what the problem is and challenge old assumptions (Weiss, 1991). For practitioners, research is not always a guide to action, but often a means of exposing personal biases and prejudices, and accessing wider experience. All kinds of research can support this process. It is important to emphasize the often serendipitous and loose nature of the relationship between research and policy in this sense, not to justify poor-quality research or an abundance of small-scale studies, but to avoid perpetuating assumptions that influence can only (and always will) be achieved through the engineering model and RCTs. This requires us to be more modest in our aspirations for evidence-informed policy (and practice) – and to be explicit about that. It also argues for a more widely shared valuing of the range of research orientations, beyond 'research for use'.

For those researchers who still wish to be more pro-active in engaging with policy, an interesting feature of the political landscape is the profile that think tanks and the like have built as policy influencers. During the New Labour era, *The Times Educational Supplement* pointed to the relative influence on policy of consultancy companies, think tanks and the higher education research community with the following claim:

> If you want to influence Labour's education policy, you could do worse than target a think tank and a management consultancy. More than London University's Institute of Education, the teaching unions or even the Labour Party, the Institute for Public Policy Research and McKinsey have the ear of people in high places.
>
> (Slater, 2005: 15)

As Denis Lawton, one-time Director of the Institute of Education, put it at the time, 'research evidence as well as the views of education theorists have too often been ignored in favour of the quick-fix bright ideas of spin doctors and advisers at No. 10' (Lawton, 2005: 142).[11] In more measured terms, Brown (2014) broadly confirms this hierarchy of influence. Relatively unencumbered by the inhibitions of the canons (and cautions) that academic research properly requires, these organizations are effective at tuning in to policy concerns and offering remedies. They are generally also good communicators and networkers in policy circles.

This might seem especially noteworthy in an era of what is sometimes referred to as 'network governance' (e.g. Ball and Junemann, 2012), where outcomes are produced by the interaction of a large number of loosely coupled actors and agencies. Certainly, the move towards a 'network governance' approach to education policymaking means that it is far from clear that impact on government is the only important avenue for researchers who wish to influence policy. Ball (2012: 9) notes that 'there are new voices within policy conversations and new conduits through which policy discourses enter policy thinking'. A review of impact studies for the 2014 REF exercise found that two of the four 'most common claims of impact related to "informing government policy" ... [and] "parliamentary scrutiny" ... [the latter being] more frequent in the social sciences' (Jump, 2015). In present circumstances, then, it may be that engagement with intermediary organizations – think tanks, consultancies, perhaps even the large education publishers and examination boards – offers another way forward.

However, many of the reservations we have expressed about the extent to which governments can accommodate research apply at least as strongly to some of these intermediary bodies. A particularly egregious example is the use that Reform made of research on teaching assistants (the Deployment and Impact of Support Staff in Schools project) to argue for a significant reduction in the number of teaching assistants (Bassett et al., 2010). In fact, the original research had criticized the lack of support for and ineffective deployment of teaching assistants, not the role per se. Our own preference, therefore, is for education researchers to do more to influence the quality of a broader public debate about education and education policy. This may even support policy influence: as Gewirtz (2003) has noted, research can influence the wider discursive milieux within which policymakers operate. If politics is as much about responding to public opinion as to research evidence, this may ultimately be the context in which research evidence should be widely available. The role of researcher as 'public intellectual' is relatively underdeveloped in English society, and particularly among education researchers these days. Yet it deserves to be given more attention. In this respect, building partnerships among different stakeholders and making use of a range of opportunities beyond the official channels to disseminate research findings can be crucial. One could even argue that this is a more democratic mode of action – attempting to influence public debate rather than seek privileged access to policy (MacDonald, 1974). Holmwood (2015) takes this a step further, in a salutary reminder of the broader project of social science: engaging the public in the circumstances of their lives and the possibilities of changing those circumstances. This is a much richer and more potentially transformative idea than that encapsulated by instrumental notions of impact, and even some variants of currently fashionable rhetoric around 'public engagement'.

The issue of research impact is thus a complex one, made more so by relatively unexamined assumptions about the value of evidence-informed policy and research for use. It is vital that in this debate proponents are clear on the realities of politics and policymaking, and clear on their aspirations. Ultimately, we suspect that all perspectives in this debate can best be served by a broad research base, and that all parties should be mindful of the challenges to the breadth of that research base, including the part that their own advocacy might play in that regard. There needs to be a place for both blue skies and critical research that is significant in disciplinary terms but whose impact on policy, if any, is an unpredictable bonus that cannot reasonably be made a condition of funding. Persuading politicians of this remains as big a challenge today as it was when David Blunkett and Charles Clarke were ministers. Yet we should continue to resist overly simplistic notions of a 'golden age' of evidence-based policy bringing education researchers into the policymaking fold.

Interestingly, in a blog post published just as this book was going to press, James Turner of The Sutton Trust and the EEF, who has been at the heart of the evidence-informed policy and practice debate, pointed to some of the limitations of the movement and called for a greater degree of realism about what could and could not be achieved. He argued that the rhetoric was 'considerably easier than the reality', that robust evaluations are 'difficult' and can produce uncomfortable results that challenge vested interests, and that 'there are significant organisational obstacles to making them happen' (Turner, 2015). He also pointed to tensions between academic researchers and those involved in the delivery of educational policy and practice, and a suspicion on the part of the latter that the former were 'more interested in indulging their academic interests than providing useful and practical results'.

Turner concluded that 'reorientating all parts of the system – from the grass roots deliverer upwards – is a massive challenge' and suggested an incremental approach to improvement. Although he himself is ultimately still attracted by a refinement of the education science model, he clearly recognizes that the grand claims of evidence-informed policy need to be replaced by more modest ambitions, at least for now. For us, though, the messy real world of educational politics he points to also justifies maintaining the diversity of education research and abandoning any expectation that a particular approach will ever be the whole story. The remainder of this book therefore looks at a range of ways in which evidence is and may be used in education policymaking in an 'imperfect' world.

Notes

[1] We made a distinction in the earlier paper (Whitty, 2006) between education research and *education* research, where the former term covered any research *about* education while the latter was applied to research *for* education, in the sense of research specifically designed for the purpose of improving the education system. We mostly use the latter term in the remainder of this chapter to indicate that we are focusing on research that seeks to influence policy and practice in education, albeit in a variety of ways. We continue to use the broader term where we refer to education research as a whole.

[2] Given the focus of this book, our prime interest here is research and policy rather than research and practice, and hence we discuss relations between researchers and policymakers rather more than we consider the equally (or more) important relationship between researchers and practitioners. The latter issue has recently been explored in, for example, *Research and the Teaching Profession: Building the capacity for a self-improving education system*

(BERA–RSA, 2014). Clearly, however, the two are not unrelated. The mantra of 'what works' has been applied to research on both policy and practice and the two are often intertwined in some of our examples, as in the National Strategies rolled out by New Labour to support school improvement, or the Education Endowment Foundation's (EEF's) toolkits and other resources designed to inform school decision-making.

[3] See https://educationendowmentfoundation.org.uk. Founded by the education charity The Sutton Trust, as lead charity in partnership with Impetus Trust (now Impetus – The Private Equity Foundation), the EEF received a founding grant of £125m from the DfE. With investment and fundraising income, the EEF intends to award as much as £200m over its 15-year lifespan.

[4] The toolkit itself resonates with the work of John Hattie and, in particular, his widely cited 2008 publication, *Visible Learning: A synthesis of over 800 meta-analyses relating to achievement.*

[5] Although impact has long been under consideration by research funders, a perceived turning point was the 2006 Warry Report, which called for much more account to be taken of the potential impact of research beyond academia, and for the research councils to deliver greater economic impact from their investments.

[6] 'Translational' research, involving the application of findings in basic science to the enhancement of health and well-being (especially in medical and nursing practice), has recently become the ideal in many circles. Lack of appropriate infrastructure is just one of the challenges it poses for research in education.

[7] For all of the criticism of the introduction of impact under the REF, this exercise is equally criticized for perpetuating a 'publish or perish' dogma within academe, inhibiting, for example, the kind of movement between academia and other sectors that would support 'useful research'. The exercise's subject-based approach is similarly felt to inhibit multidisciplinary research – the cause of which is currently to the fore as the perceived best prospect for addressing societal challenges. The REF's focus on instrumental impact via single projects may also be at odds with research users' need for syntheses of research findings to provide the 'state-of-the-art' knowledge in a given field.

[8] This is not to say that there is room for complacency. Education also saw one of the highest proportions of 1* (less esteemed) research (7 per cent, versus an average of 3 per cent across the other units of assessment). Equally, education's result was bolstered by relatively high scores for 'impact' (42.9 per cent) and 'environment' (48.4 per cent) as opposed to those for the rigour, originality and significance of its outputs (21.7 per cent). Increased selectivity in the number of staff entered for the exercise also played its part: only 27 per cent of eligible staff working in education were returned – the lowest proportion of any unit of assessment. The particular history of education departments in terms of their absorption of teachers as teacher educators, and the polarization with regard to research activity between those institutions delivering teacher education at scale and those not, provides some explanation for this selectivity (BERA, 2015).

[9] See, for example, Wilkes (2014) for a detailed insight into the complexities of policymaking. Cassen *et al.* (2015: 9), in a book that promotes the use of research evidence in policymaking, are appropriately realistic about what it can achieve, noting that 'evidence is far from the only force guiding policy – in fact it is sometimes completely absent'.

[10] We do not know why; it is possible that there were questions over its robustness, but that was not stated at the time.

[11] There are, of course, more positive examples. Within its own field, The Sutton Trust is a good example of a charitable organization that takes academic research seriously while having the ear of government. However, it is predominantly an advocacy body and this determines what research it funds and publishes.

Chapter 2

Ideology and evidence in English teacher education

Introduction

A good example of some of the difficulties of developing evidence-based policies discussed in the previous chapter is the case of teacher education in England. Teacher education has long been identified as in need of reform but evidence to support that contention has been lacking, especially since the 1980s when the then Conservative Government of Margaret Thatcher established a Council for the Accreditation of Teacher Education (CATE) to review all initial teacher training providers in England and recommend whether they should receive accreditation to provide courses leading to Qualified Teacher Status (QTS). Her Majesty's Inspectorate of Schools (HMI) (subsequently Ofsted) was charged with reporting to CATE on the quality of provision, a role that has been significantly expanded over the subsequent 30 years under successive governments. From 1992 onwards, a succession of sets of competences and standards for courses to develop in their trainees were drawn up by governments and the Teacher Training Agency (and its successor bodies), and there was increasing emphasis on the time all trainees needed to spend in school. At the same time, a number of new routes to QTS were introduced (see Furlong *et al.*, 2000; Furlong, 2013).

When the New Labour Government left office in 2010, there were three main routes into school teaching in England. All led to Qualified Teacher Status (QTS), which (with some limited exceptions) was a requirement for anyone teaching in a publicly maintained school, including most academies:

- Partnerships led by higher education institutions (HEIs)
  These provided both undergraduate and postgraduate qualifications. The former included three- and four-year BEd and BA(QTS) courses. The number of undergraduate trainees had decreased from 9,770 in 1998/9 to 7,620 in 2007/8. Most trainees, around 27,000 a year, therefore undertook one-year postgraduate courses: the Postgraduate Certificate in Education (PGCE) at Masters level or the Professional Graduate Certificate in Education (PgCE) below Masters level.

- School-centred initial teacher training schemes (SCITTs)
  These were consortia of schools that offered training towards the PGCE. They accounted for around 5 per cent of trainees per year. In SCITTs, the consortium

itself arranged the training and channelled the funding for placements, whereas in HEI-led partnerships the university arranged placements and channelled the funding to schools. Nevertheless, universities validated the SCITTs' PGCEs.

- Employment-based initial teacher training (EBITT)
  EBITTs involved 'on-the-job' training and fell into three groups: the Graduate Teacher Programme (GTP), Overseas Trained Teacher Programme (OTTP) and TeachFirst, a scheme to bring high-flying new graduates into teaching in challenging schools. They all led to Qualified Teacher Status (QTS) and some, including TeachFirst after some initial hesitation, also led to a PGCE, an identical qualification to the other routes.

In total, in 2009/10, there were 234 providers offering routes into teaching, including 75 HEI-led partnerships, 59 SCITTs and 100 EBITTs. However, some of these providers had a very small number of trainees. HEIs were responsible for the vast majority of trainees: in 2009/10, for example, they trained 78.7 per cent of the recruits to teacher training programmes, compared with 16.7 per cent in EBITTs and 5.6 per cent in SCITTs.

With regard to the quality of the training provided at that time, Ofsted judged that 90 per cent of provision was 'good' or better. Between 2008 and 2011, during Christine Gilbert's time as Her Majesty's Chief Inspector (HMCI), 49 per cent of HEI-led partnerships, 36 per cent of SCITTs and 18 per cent of EBITTs were rated 'outstanding' by Ofsted, so the evidence at that time suggested that HEI-led partnerships provided higher quality training than school-led partnerships and employment-based routes (HMCI, 2011). Although Smithers and Robinson (2011) rightly pointed out that, of the top ten providers during the same period, four were SCITTs, four were university-led partnerships and two were EBITTs, large differences in scale and cost meant that HEI-led partnerships still trained the vast majority of students on these highly-rated programmes and were the most cost-effective in doing so.

Whether or not it was true to claim that British society or the English school system was broken, it is hard to argue on this evidence that the teacher training system was broken when the New Labour Government left office. Quality was not manifestly poor, despite what we were often led to believe by some politicians and popular newspapers. On the contrary, it had only recently been claimed, on the basis of the sort of evidence presented above, that England had some of the best-qualified and best-trained teachers ever (House of Commons, 2010).

Coalition and Conservative government reforms

However, there were those who argued, not unreasonably, that standards were still not good enough compared to the country's leading competitors internationally. In this vein, in 2010, the incoming Secretary of State for Education, Michael Gove, and the new Chief Inspector, Sir Michael Wilshaw, decided that things needed to change. The latter also expressed some doubts about the rigour of previous Ofsted inspections of initial teacher education and, following consultation on a new framework for teacher training inspection, significantly raised the threshold for courses to be awarded an 'outstanding' grade. Those with less than a 'good' grade were put on notice to make rapid improvements or lose accreditation. Further revisions were made to the Ofsted framework for the inspection of initial teacher education in 2012 and 2014.

The Coalition Government's 2010 White Paper on *The Importance of Teaching* had already encouraged more school-led initial teacher training in England, including the creation of around 500 Teaching Schools, the latter being those rated by Ofsted as outstanding in teaching and learning and with the potential to take over leadership of teacher training from the universities. The extent, scale and speed of this proposed takeover remained unclear, but there was no doubt that this was the direction of travel favoured by the government and that some Conservative ministers would have liked – and would still like – to see more than half of new teachers trained on school-led routes.

The key policy for realizing this change was School Direct, a scheme which, in simple terms, involved the allocation of training places to schools, who then cashed in places with a university or other accredited ITT provider to deliver a training package for a teacher whom the school was subsequently expected to employ, although that particular requirement has since been watered down. Trainees filling a vacancy could be paid a salary, as under the earlier EBITT arrangements, but most were to be funded by loans and bursaries as in conventional HEI-led provision.

When the School Direct policy was first announced, it was proposed to be restricted to about 500 places and was designed to meet teacher supply needs that were not being met through existing mechanisms. Subsequently, it has been reinvented as the main means for putting schools in the lead in teacher training and making HEIs more responsive to the needs of schools. Its projected share of allocated postgraduate trainee numbers was increased to over 9,000 for 2013/14, rising to over 17,000 for 2015/16, as shown in Table 2.1 below.

Table 2.1: Postgraduate teacher trainee enrolments

	2011/12	2012/13	2013/14	2014/15	2015/16
HE provider	28,669	28,841	26,790	23,095	22,224
School Direct	0	772	9,586	15,254	17,609

Source: Figures as cited in Roberts and Foster (2015).

Even though, in these allocations of teacher training numbers, HEI-led partnerships still had a majority of places, some individual HEIs lost virtually all their core numbers and many were becoming dependent on gaining School Direct contracts for survival. However, the overall allocation figures were inflated by government to enable School Direct to grow where it could while allowing HEIs to maintain a presence in case the new approach failed to meet teacher supply needs. In practice, School Direct grew rapidly in some subjects and regions but not in others. In 2015, the new Conservative Government abandoned the allocation system and proposed that all providers could recruit as many trainees as they wished until a national cap on numbers was reached. How this will result in meeting teacher supply needs has not so far been explained. Nevertheless, it seems to represent a further move away from centralized workforce planning towards a more marketized approach.

As a result of all these changes, the landscape of initial teacher education has become even more varied than it was in 2010. Although there is some dispute about what constitutes a 'route', a 'course' or a 'qualification', and what is merely a 'funding mechanism', the Association of School and College Leaders (ASCL) identified what it called the following 'Routes into Teaching' in 2015:

- **SCITT: http://tinyurl.com/k2wblyv**
  Led by a network of schools that have been given powers to run their own training independently.
  Course generally lasts a year.

- **School Direct (unsalaried): http://tinyurl.com/lx8fw46**
  Designed by a group of schools in partnership with a university or SCITT with the schools themselves recruiting.
  Generally lasts a year.

- **School Direct (salaried): http://tinyurl.com/mxuxpy8**
  As above.
  Earn a salary while training; school covers the cost of achieving QTS.

- **Teach First: http://tinyurl.com/mgswvba**
  Earn while you train and work in a challenging school in a low-income community.
  Minimum 2.1 degree.
  Two-year course.

- **Troops to Teachers: http://tinyurl.com/ol8pxau**
  For military personnel in the two years before or the two years after leaving the Armed Forces.
  With a degree: one-year course through SD unsalaried, salaried or university-led PGCE.
  Without a degree: two-year, school-based, salaried teacher training programme.

- **Researchers in Schools: http://tinyurl.com/lfxm4rt**
  For researchers who have completed or are finishing their doctorate. Two-year salaried programme in six regions.

- **Undergraduate route: http://tinyurl.com/kvmaf7d**
  Study for a degree and teacher training at the same time. Minimum C at GCSE in English and maths (plus science for primary or Key Stage 3) and 2 A-levels (check with individual universities).
  Full time 3–4 years; part time 4–6 years.

- **Postgraduate route (PGCE): http://tinyurl.com/ofl2jjz**
  If you already have a degree, one-year course at a university or college, with school placements.

(adapted from annex to ASCL, 2015)[1]

Small wonder that a review of initial teacher education conducted by Andrew Carter for the Coalition Government during 2014 concluded that the system had become 'complex' and information about it 'confusing'. The review therefore called for clearer information about choices on official websites, and recommended the development of a 'framework of core ITT content' (Carter, 2015).

Overall, however, the review was less critical of the status quo, and perhaps more in favour of greater regulation of the market than may have been expected by Secretary of State Gove when he set it up. Reporting after he had been replaced by the apparently more conciliatory Nicky Morgan, it concluded that the quality of ITT was generally good and gave examples of strengths across different routes and different forms of partnership. Although some university-based teacher educators felt threatened by its view that, while Qualified Teacher Status was essential, an academic qualification like the PGCE should be optional for teachers, others were encouraged by the report's espousal of 'evidence-based teaching'.

Even policymakers committed to reform have been unclear about how far the move towards school-led teacher training should go. In their public pronouncements, ministers had generally favoured the continued involvement of universities in all routes, although Nick Gibb, a junior minister, had previously implied that this might only be through the accreditation of qualifications (House of Commons, 2012). By 2015, however, this was in doubt as Conservative and Liberal Democrat ministers failed to agree on how to respond to the aforementioned Carter Report's suggestion that the PCGE should be optional (Carter, 2015).

On assuming office in 2010, the Coalition Government had proposed setting up a small number of University Training Schools with three core functions of teaching children, training teachers and undertaking research. These seem to have been inspired directly by the Finnish model but are, like the Finnish system as a whole, arguably out of step with the main thrust of British Government policy, which is to put schools rather than universities firmly in the lead. In the event, only two such schools have in fact been established – a secondary school at the University of Birmingham and a primary school at Cambridge – and a proposal for such a school from the Institute of Education in London was turned down by ministers amid charges of political bias (Mansell, 2014).

However, while Conservative ministers have been at best ambivalent about the role of universities in teacher education, the House of Commons Select Committee for Education came out in 2012 much more strongly in favour of a continuing role for universities in teacher education partnerships, arguing that 'a diminution of universities' [current] role in teacher training could bring considerable demerits' and cautioning specifically against it. Furthermore, they argued that training should 'include theoretical and research elements [as well as significant school experience] … as in the best systems internationally and [indeed] much [current] provision here' (House of Commons, 2012: 32).

The government had never provided a formal response to similar comments in the previous committee's 2010 report on teacher education – and that may have been one of the reasons why the new committee chose to return to the subject in 2012. But select committees have limited influence; much more significant is the stance of the government itself and its agencies. Under New Labour, the Training and Development Agency for Schools (TDA), successor to the Teacher Training Agency (TTA) first established by a Conservative Government in 1994, was the 'national agency and recognised sector body responsible for the training and development of the school workforce', including teachers. From April 2012, the functions of the TDA and some of those of the simultaneously abolished General Teaching Council for England were taken back into the government Department for Education (DfE) in a newly formed executive agency called the Teaching Agency. Then, in April 2013, the Teaching Agency was merged with the National College for School Leadership to form a new super-agency within the DfE called the National College for Teaching and Leadership.

While many took these developments to demonstrate that the government was taking more direct control over teacher training, the truth was, of course, that governments of various political hues have controlled teacher training quite tightly for many years, albeit through arm's-length bodies. Trusting teachers, let alone teacher educators, has not been at the heart of British Government policy since the 1988 Education Reform Act, although in the past decade there has been more rhetoric from all governments about handing power back to the professionals – or at least to schools and their head teachers.[2] This is all consistent with the combination of state control and market forces that has dominated English school policies now for several decades (Whitty, 1989; Whitty *et al.*, 1998) and, as I shall indicate in what follows, there have been parallel developments in relation to teacher training.

Geoff Whitty

Making sense of changes in teacher training policy

In a somewhat schematic characterization of the recent history of English schooling (Barber, 2005), Michael Barber, former professor of education, government advisor, McKinsey Partner and then a special advisor to the Chief Executive of Pearson, described the period prior to 1979 as one of 'uninformed professionalism' in which unbridled teacher autonomy reigned. This, he argued, was replaced under Margaret Thatcher's government by 'uninformed prescription' or dubious practice imposed from above.

When I think about my own experience of teacher education from the early 1970s to the turn of the century, governments certainly moved away from trusting the teacher trainers to providing increasingly detailed central prescription. As far as I can remember, when I took up my first job as a teacher educator at the University of Bath in 1973, I was left entirely to my own devices in deciding what I should teach my students on the Postgraduate Certificate in Education course. Although we had an area training organization and associate tutors in schools, the course content was entirely determined by university staff and we were definitely in the lead.

The first significant change came after 1984 with the establishment of CATE – the Council for the Accreditation of Teacher Education – that assessed all courses of teacher training against nationally defined requirements and all higher education institutions engaged in teacher education for the schools sector were inspected by HMI against those requirements (DES, 1984). Over the years those requirements became increasingly detailed and expressed as competences and then standards that had to be met by all students awarded Qualified Teacher Status. From 1992 onwards, all university-led courses had to be run in formal partnerships with schools and a number of new routes to Qualified Teacher Status were introduced, including some led by schools rather than universities. It was also around this time that Ofsted and the then TTA were created. The percentage of teachers trained on alternative routes increased from about 2 per cent in 1997 to 20 per cent in 2009, while trainees on all routes, including HEI-led partnerships, became school-based for the majority of the time.

Barber (2005) claimed that, in the period after 1997, Tony Blair's New Labour Government, to whom he was the chief advisor on school standards and effectiveness, heralded an era of 'informed prescription'. In teacher education his claim was that research on what works informed the TDA's teaching standards and Ofsted inspection criteria as well as the National Strategies for literacy and numeracy, which had improved the system as a whole. However, he implied that, as a result of the re-education of teachers (and teacher trainers) through these national policies, the government would soon be able to relax central controls and rely instead on the 'informed professionalism' of teachers. This rhetoric was evident in the final years

Ideology and evidence in English teacher education

of New Labour and even more strongly in the pronouncements of the subsequent Coalition and Conservative governments.

Yet it is not quite as simple as Barber's typology suggests. In fact, as implied earlier, we can see in teacher training policy yet another example of the contemporary policy preference for a combination of the strong state and the free market (Gamble, 1994). In the current teaching standards and Ofsted inspection criteria, we now have a somewhat narrower prescribed core requirement than before, but even greater prescription and policing of its detail in relation to specifics like the teaching of reading by phonics and the management of pupil behaviour. This constitutes the official 'national' professionalism, as I have put it.

But true to the marketizing approach to the reform of the school system, there will now be more autonomy beyond that prescribed core, as autonomous schools are encouraged to take on more responsibilities for teacher training. Back in 2000, I had predicted that we would see the emergence of a variety of 'local' professionalisms associated with individual schools or consortia of schools:

> To some degree, schools and teachers appear to have been 'empowered' to develop their own 'local' professionalisms. On the other hand, centrally specified competences and standards mean that local professional freedom is actually quite tightly constrained by the demands of the 'evaluative state'.
> (Whitty, 2000)

In practice, in the years immediately following that claim, it was the constraints of the evaluative state that came to dominate under the Blair Government. In this connection, Furlong (2008) has argued that, while Blair's legacy included some positive aspects for teachers, they were also 'much more managed than in the past', suggesting that powerful mechanisms had been put in place to ensure that teachers, in their day-to-day practice, would 'conform to the centrally prescribed policy agendas and strategies, whether or not they agreed with them' (Furlong, 2008: 736–7). Yet Furlong also pointed out that some of the world's leading education systems were now adopting less constrained versions of teacher professionalism. For example, Singapore's adoption of a more open form of teacher professionalism in its 'thinking schools' raised some doubts in his mind about whether the highly regulated New Labour approach was entirely appropriate for a twenty-first-century profession.

As I suggested earlier, there has since been some easing of direct central control, at least at the margins, even in the English context, so the prospect of more 'local professionalisms' is again on the agenda despite the backtracking during the Blair years. However, it is far from clear how or in what sense these 'local professionalisms' will be *informed* professionalisms, to use Barber's term. If, as Conservative ministers sometimes imply, professional wisdom lies exclusively in schools, university-generated research on teaching and learning may not be regarded as having a significant contribution to make to the professional formation of teachers. An extreme version of this position was stated by Michael Gove just before he was moved away from the Education portfolio:

> In the past, the education debate has been dominated by education academics – which is why so much of the research and evidence on how children actually learn has been so poor. Now, thankfully, teachers are taking control of their profession's intellectual life, taking the lead in pioneering educational research and creating a living evidence base.
>
> (Gove, 2013b)

Even Gove, however, conceded that 'the best higher education institutions welcome our changes because they know that discriminating schools will increasingly choose partners in HE who deliver the best quality training and development', citing his alma mater Oxford University as an example (Gove, 2013b).

Meanwhile, there has been an additional development. This is what I have termed 'branded' professionalisms, drawing upon a literature that explores how knowledge-intensive firms like Deloitte use their brand as a platform for a common identity and consistent expectations (Elliott, 2008). In education, autonomous schools, or academies in the English case, are increasingly being linked into chains, like the ARK[3] and Harris academy chains, which are seeking also to take on more responsibilities for teacher training either by becoming accredited providers themselves or by franchising other providers, including universities, to train the particular sorts of teachers they want. So we will have distinctive ARK teachers or Harris teachers, alongside an existing example of 'branded professionalism' in the case of Teach First teachers. In some ways, the concept may even be a throwback in that, for example, we have had Froebel teachers in the past. Some might claim that nowadays we have Oxford University interns with recognizable characteristics, and interestingly this was the example that Gove cited favourably above, but few if any other universities have yet succeeded in branding their teachers in this way.

Although there is no reason why leading universities could not be among the new 'branded professionalisms', it is noteworthy that in the USA one of the strongest examples of branded professionalism is the Relay Graduate School of Education (Relay GSE), a collaboration by three charter management organizations (the equivalent of English academy chains), which explicitly positions itself as a response to 'a nationwide failure by most university-based teacher education programs to prepare teachers for the realities of the 21st century classroom' (Relay GSE, 2013). There are also some other parallels in the trend towards the marketization of teacher preparation in the USA (T. Arnett, 2015). However, deregulation has so far been much less significant than in England, not least because charter schools (the equivalent of English free schools and academies) make up a much lower proportion of provision and, in most states, are more subject to government regulation. A more radical proposal to deregulate entry to teaching, from Scott Walker, the Republican

Governor of Wisconsin, has been watered down in response to widespread public opposition (Beck, 2015).

Future prospects for English teacher education

So where might all this be leading? David Bell, former Permanent Secretary at the DfE, has offered his own reflections on the English school reforms of recent decades. He suggested that we were probably moving towards a 'system of many small systems' in English education:

> 'Messiness' in terms of structures will be a natural by-product of radical structural reform as we move from a standardised national system to a system of many small systems. I don't have a single solution to offer, nor do I necessarily think there should be one, as the end-point of these school reforms hasn't been reached yet.
>
> (Bell, 2012)

He was thinking here of small systems of schools in particular, including academy chains, a few effective local authorities and federations of schools led by Teaching Schools or successful individual school leaders. Interestingly, his use of the term 'messiness' resonates with Stephen Ball's characterization of post-modern educational systems (Ball, 2011b). He did not specifically refer to teacher education but it will be clear from my analysis above that teacher education may itself be moving towards a system of small systems of the sort Bell envisages.

However, there is an even more extreme scenario, which may be the eventual endpoint of the developments described by Bell. The Coalition Government decided that its new free schools would not have to employ qualified teachers and could instead employ whomever head teachers regard as most suitable. It subsequently made a similar change for academies, which now constitute a majority of all secondary schools in England and an increasing proportion of primary schools. Thus, the officially prescribed training requirement discussed above will apply to a diminishing number of schools in future, as will the National Curriculum. There has also been a significant deregulation of training requirements in the post-compulsory education sector. So this could be just the start of a deregulation of teacher education, effectively ending even the core national professionalism associated with the pre-service award of QTS, and leaving teacher supply and teacher quality to market forces.

Meanwhile, a requirement on the Secretary of State to plan the teaching workforce has been quietly removed from the statute book, and the head of the National College for Teaching and Leadership suggested at the 2013 North of England Conference that such planning should be left to localities:

> In the future I would like to see local areas deciding on the numbers of teachers they will need each year rather than a fairly arbitrary figure

passed down from the Department for Education. I have asked my officials ... to work with schools, academy chains and local authorities to help them to devise their own local teacher supply model. I don't think Whitehall should be deciding that nationally we need 843 geography teachers, when a more accurate figure can be worked out locally.

(Taylor, 2013)

In that case, of course, there would effectively be no overall system of small systems – just schools and families of schools, an echo of Mrs Thatcher's alleged comment that there was no such thing as society, just individual men and women and families (Thatcher, quoted in Keay, 1987).

It is probably not a coincidence, then, that this is the very scenario favoured in the 1980s and early 1990s by New Right pamphleteers of both neo-liberal and neo-conservative varieties. As I said at the time, in my inaugural lecture at Goldsmiths College in May 1991:

The neo-conservatives regard most of the existing curriculum of teacher training as dispensable, so in their ideal world the prescribed curriculum would only be a good dose of 'proper subject knowledge'. The neo-liberals would allow schools to go into the market and recruit whomever they wanted, but would expect them in practice to favour pure graduates ... over those who have 'suffered' from teacher training ...

There is general agreement amongst both groups that, say, two or three years of subject study in a conventional vein is sufficient academic preparation for would-be teachers and any training necessary can be done on an apprenticeship basis in schools.

(Whitty, 1991: 5)

I also suggested that one of the reasons why some members of the New Right could believe, at one and the same time, in permitting the entry into teaching of people with little or no training, while imposing increasingly stringent criteria upon the content of established routes into teacher training, lay in its belief that there were 'enemies within'. At one level this was a general argument about producer interests, but it was also a more specific attack on the alleged ideological bias of teacher educators. Indeed, a recurring theme in the pamphlets of the New Right pressure groups at that time was the need to rid the system of the liberal or left educational establishment, which was seen to have been behind the 'progressive collapse' of the English educational system and that, 'prey to ideology and self-interest, is no longer in touch with the public' (Hillgate Group, 1987: 10). It was therefore 'time to set aside ... the professional educators and the majority of organised teacher unions ... [who] are primarily responsible for the present state of Britain's schools' (Hillgate Group, 1987, cited in Whitty, 1991: 6).

Twenty years later, of course, the attack came not from New Right think tanks but from a government minister, Michael Gove, who seems to have learned the script. Indeed, he employed similar rhetoric to those earlier pamphleteers in an extraordinary attack in the *Daily Mail* on so-called Marxist teachers and teacher educators, whom he characterized as 'the enemies of promise' (Gove, 2013a). Nick Gibb, who has similar views, has now been given the responsibility for teacher training in the majority Conservative Government elected in 2015, and among his early acts was the appointment of Anthony O'Hear, one of the New Right pamphleteers of the 1980s (O'Hear, 1988), to the 'independent expert group' to advise on content of teacher education courses (DfE, 2015). Other contemporary commentators on the right have gone even further. Again echoing earlier claims from the New Right pamphleteers that aspects of teacher education courses can be 'harmful' (Dawson, 1981) or 'undermining' (Lawlor, 1990), Charles Moore has asked in *The Spectator*:

> Why not introduce a rule which states that no one with a formal teaching qualification is allowed to teach in any school unless he or she can prove compensatory qualifications from other fields? These could include having worked for at least two years in a private-sector job, or served in the armed forces or possessing an honours degree from a Russell Group university. After quite a short time, no one would want to apply for formal teaching qualifications any more and the whole system which has guaranteed mediocrity and worse in the state system for 50 years would fall apart.
> (Moore, 2013)

In that same inaugural lecture back in 1991, I drew attention to some flaws in the New Right argument even from their own position, pointing out that, if their critique of teacher training was right, schools surely needed to be purged of teachers who had 'suffered' from teacher training before they could themselves be entrusted with teacher training. Furthermore, I pointed to the practical problems of handing all initial teacher training over to the schools, arguing that such a shift would involve significant changes in the structure of the teaching profession and the culture of schooling at a time when schools were already having difficulty coping with existing educational reforms.

Although some may argue that these considerations still apply today, a lot has changed in teacher education in the last 20 years. Many of the more legitimate criticisms of university-led teacher training have already been addressed through constructive engagement between government, universities and schools. I argued in 1991 that higher education institutions should actively embrace school-based training and partnership working, and most have subsequently welcomed multiple training routes and worked ever more closely with schools. And, inconvenient a truth as it may be, some university departments of education were involved right from the start in the development of Teach First, one of the teacher training routes consistently praised by government ministers, including Michael Gove.

Yet current policies are being rolled out in a manner that risks losing from the system some of the best HEI practice that has developed in recent years. Cuts in secondary ITT numbers have already impacted upon many HEIs and most institutions are in the future likely to face cuts in core numbers as a result of the new and more demanding Ofsted inspection framework and the increasing emphasis on school-led training routes. The biggest impact is likely to come from the rapid roll-out of School Direct. Even if overall numbers allocated to HEIs by one means or another are retained, the volatility of funding from year to year and between different subjects and universities could be quite considerable. The actual implementation of School Direct has also been problematic – as has been clear from a number of reports in the *Times Educational Supplement* (e.g. Maddern, 2013).

Many of the official pronouncements about the move to school-led training have misrepresented the nature and quality of existing HEI-school partnerships. For example, the first results under a new inspection framework for teacher training were described in an Ofsted press release, issued the same week as the announcement of a tranche of new Teaching Schools, as evidence of the superiority of school-led routes. In its original form, later amended on the website (Ofsted, 2013a), the Ofsted press release included spurious interpretations of limited data and at least one factual error and omitted to mention anything that reflected well on HEIs or badly on school-led teacher training schemes.

A report in *The Times* at that time suggested that HMCI Sir Michael Wilshaw saw a connection between the allegedly inferior teacher training inspection results from HEIs and a letter from 100 education academics attacking the government's National Curriculum (Hurst, 2013). Regardless of the strength of their arguments, many of the signatories to that letter were retired and very few were involved in the design or delivery of initial teacher training, so could hardly be held responsible for the quality of current teacher training programmes. Whether or not Ofsted's own stance was politically motivated, as implied by the Universities' Council for the Education of Teachers (UCET, 2013), there is much to suggest that the Conservative-led Coalition Government's policy on teacher education was ideologically driven rather than informed by evidence about the quality of training in different routes, despite that same government's avowed commitment to evidence-informed policy referred to in Chapter 1 (Goldacre, 2013).

Nevertheless, it seems to me unlikely that extreme deregulation will prevail, particularly if current ministers move on. My own expectation is that the future of teacher education in England will fall closer to that implied in a question that Graham Stuart, Conservative Chair of the Education Select Committee, put to a witness who appeared before his Committee in 2011. He asked:

Ideology and evidence in English teacher education

> [M]ight we not see a concentration of fewer, higher-quality, more assured HEIs? Aren't there rather a lot at the moment, and some of them are pretty dubious on economics, viability and other issues? May we not see a consolidation at one level of HEIs, while spreading the engagement of schools? That is the Government vision, isn't it?
>
> (House of Commons Education Select Committee, 2011)

Certainly, the chances of initial teacher education being maintained in all current higher education institutions are remote. Some will leave the scene as a result of judgements about their quality or the impact of competition, but this is unlikely to be the only consequence of current policies. It is also likely that some research-intensive universities will decide, as one witness hinted at that same Select Committee hearing, that the new arrangements for university involvement in ITE may prove just too onerous to justify remaining in that area of work. The transaction and opportunity costs entailed may put at risk other elements of their work, including high-quality research. The University of Bath was the first research-led university with an Outstanding Ofsted grade for its teacher training provision to announce its withdrawal – against my own advice to its Vice-Chancellor, as it happens – and it was shortly followed by the Open University. Meanwhile, Warwick University separated its teacher training work from other aspects of educational studies. Other universities are monitoring the situation carefully, while some providers such as Anglia Ruskin University have withdrawn for other reasons.

At a conference in January 2013, I predicted that, as a result of the developments discussed here, some English higher education institutions would abandon teacher education, some would embrace School Direct with enthusiasm, private 'for-profit' providers as well as academy chains would enter the field and compete nationally, some education research and education studies degrees would move to social science departments, some key 'full-service' education departments would remain in universities and new institutional, regional, national and international partnerships would develop (Whitty, 2013). Most of these things have since happened, including the entry of Hibernia College Dublin into the online teacher training market in England, albeit with limited success.

Writing after the June 2015 announcement that schools and ITT providers will be able, subject to an overall national limit, to recruit as many trainees as they wish in 2016/17, *Schools Week* reported comments from Chris Husbands, my successor as director of the IOE, that this would be likely to lead to a further expansion of Schools Direct and a further decline in university-led provision. Husbands said in his blog:

> The immediate likelihood is the further expansion, despite the challenges, of School Direct. The recent hints are that school and school group bidding for School Direct places for 2016–2017 will account for the vast majority of [initial teacher education], with very loose regional monitoring

of demand. Essentially, this means higher education allocations will be residual, mopping up numbers not allocated to schools, which is in turn likely to be the hard to recruit areas. It's unlikely higher status universities will remain in this highly uncertain market for long, which means the de facto transfer of teacher supply to several thousand competing small businesses. Recent evidence suggests that the outcomes are likely to be unpredictable.

(Husbands, quoted in Scott, 2015)

If teacher supply is to be threatened by an ideologically driven policy in this way, there is an urgent need at least to put some evidence into the public domain. So, although the government itself has been reluctant to cite the evidence on which its policies are based, my colleagues at Bath Spa University are seeking funding for a project to establish whether or not the government's apparent preference for school-led teacher training routes can be justified by the quality of the teachers they produce.

Researching Diversity in Teacher Education (DiTE)

There is certainly a major policy debate to be had nationally – and indeed internationally – about the efficacy of different approaches to teacher education in the light of the challenges of preparing teachers for twenty-first century schools. In its crudest terms this has often been reduced to a binary opposition of university-led versus school-led approaches to the training of teachers. Yet, within this apparent binary are important ethical, conceptual and empirical questions about the nature of professional formation, the governance of the sector, the balance between theoretical and practical knowledge and arguments about the best ways to ensure teacher supply, teacher quality and the achievement of desired outcomes.

In England, as we have seen, the teacher education sector now embraces a wide range of routes into teaching, which may have differential implications for teacher selection, the structure of professional learning, the leadership of the sector, the efficiency of the system and its outcomes for schools and their students. It is important that these implications can be explored empirically and understood. However, as indicated above, advocacy of the different models of teacher education is too often driven by ideological commitments rather than by evidence of their effects, so there is an urgent need to bring robust research to bear on the issues identified here. The DiTE project currently under development at Bath Spa University is seeking to do just that, as are related projects at the University of Birmingham and at the IOE and the Institute of Fiscal Studies.[4]

The project for which Bath Spa University is seeking funding is loosely modelled on the Modes of Teacher Education (MOTE) project that I led at the Institute of Education in the 1990s in collaboration with colleagues at the Universities of Sheffield and Bristol and Homerton College, Cambridge (Furlong et al., 2000). The new project will produce a new topography of routes to qualified teacher status in England, updating and adding to the topographies produced for the earlier research project (Barrett *et al.*, 1992; Whiting *et al.*, 1996). The topography will cover such dimensions as the duration, level, cost, location and leadership of the provision, and the demographic characteristics of the tutors and students involved in the different routes to Qualified Teacher Status (QTS).

A second phase of the project will involve in-depth exploration of the characteristics of a sample of different types of provision in terms of their aims, structure, qualifications and, most crucially, the student experience. The sample will include HEI-led partnerships offering BA(QTS) and PGCE courses, SCITT schemes, Teach First provision, School Direct and School Direct salaried routes and the Troops to Teachers programme, and also perhaps those following the Assessment Only route to QTS, including unqualified teachers recruited directly to academies or free schools. The study will consider how the different routes conceptualize the professional knowledge required by teachers and how trainee teachers are introduced to that knowledge, as well as whether the workplace functions differently as a site of professional learning on the different routes.

A third component of the project will entail specifying and measuring any differential outcomes and effects of the different training routes studied in Phase 2. This was something that was attempted by the earlier MOTE study, which examined whether different routes produced different teaching competences and/or different professional attitudes. However, this aspect of the work will need to be reconceptualized and taken further to establish more clearly which competences and characteristics are developed within the school-based and HEI-based aspects of provision. The DiTE project may also try to explore some new issues, such as whether there are different rates of employment from different routes and whether teachers trained on different routes have differential effects on students' learning outcomes. This sort of research is currently being pursued in the USA but is proving technically challenging and politically controversial, especially in its attempts to utilize value added models (VAM) to assess the impact of teachers trained by different institutions on pupil performance (Mathis, 2012).

Finally, it is intended that the Bath Spa project will contribute to a broader understanding of processes of professional formation in teaching (and potentially allow comparisons with other professions). It could involve analyses of changes in the nature of professional formation for teaching by making comparisons with the findings of the MOTE project in the 1990s and with some comparative studies being planned elsewhere. The study will also have implications for policy on the education and training of teachers and it may go on to develop specific policy proposals, possibly in association with civil society partners such as think tanks.

Although this research proposal as a whole may prove difficult to fund in the climate discussed in Chapter 1, we are proceeding with some of its elements on a limited scale in the belief that the public debate around policy is better informed by some credible research evidence rather than none.

Such research on the nature and impact of different approaches to teacher education may help to move that public debate towards issues that are less defined by political grandstanding. Already to one side of the parochial debates in England about the institutional location and leadership of teacher education, there is a potentially much more constructive debate about how best to prepare teachers for contemporary schools in terms of the relationship between theory and practice. Much of this has been stimulated by international discourse about 'clinical practice' models of teacher preparation. OECD (2010), for example, argued that:

> the best-performing countries are working to move their initial teacher-education programmes towards a model based less on preparing academics and more on preparing professionals in clinical settings, in which they get into schools earlier, spend more time there and get more and better support in the process.
>
> (OECD, 2010: 238)

Michael Gove (2013b) suggested that such approaches involve giving aspiring teachers 'the opportunity to work in a great school from day one, just like student medics in hospitals – learning from more experienced colleagues and immediately putting their new skills into practice'. However, not only did this somewhat misrepresent the nature of medical training, it also ignored the extent to which the best such programmes entail not just 'clinical practice', but 'research-informed clinical practice'. Indeed, in the same document cited above, OECD (2010: 239) itself pointed out that 'some countries, notably Shanghai-China and Finland, provide teachers with the research skills needed to enable them to improve their practice in a highly disciplined way'. This is one of the ways in which research literacy might be better incorporated into teacher education wherever it is located, as was argued in a recent report from the British Educational Research Association and the Royal Society of Arts. Significantly, that report concludes by calling for 'an end to the false dichotomy between HE and school-based approaches to initial teacher education' (BERA-RSA, 2014).[5]

Notes

[1] Given who it represents, it is perhaps understandable that ASCL lists school-led schemes first, but it may also suggest that the government's agenda of representing school-led approaches as mainstream and HEI-led schemes as residual is having an effect.

[2] The Conservatives have generally been less enthusiastic about a collective professional voice for teachers and, in one of his first acts on becoming Secretary of State in 2010, Michael Gove abolished the General Teaching Council for England (GTCE). However, as this book was going to press, ministers in the new Conservative administration expressed limited support for a proposed new College of Teaching, as a voluntary membership body owned by teachers

themselves. Labour had expressed support for a rather stronger version of this body in the run-up to the 2015 general election.

[3] ARK originally stood for Absolute Returns for Kids.

[4] The latter project has already produced one report: Allen *et al.* (2014).

[5] It should be noted that I was involved in the inquiry that led to that report. However, we are not alone in making the point that it is the nature of the programme rather than its institutional provenance that is important here. A recent report on successful clinical practice models in the USA includes university and non-university based programmes (UTRU, 2015). I am currently involved in a research project at Teachers College, Columbia University, exploring how we might we articulate and measure the effects that 'research-rich' programmes have on teachers' professional formation. Other collaborative 'clinical practice' models are being developed and evaluated in other parts of the world, notably Quality Teaching Rounds in Australia (see Gore and Bowe, 2015).

Chapter 3
The (mis)use of evidence in policy borrowing
A transatlantic case study

Introduction

International policy tourism and policy borrowing in education have become common occurrences. They are now worldwide phenomena, but the focus in this chapter is on transatlantic policy exchanges, as these have a particularly long history and are also particularly important today. They are used here as a case study, which in Stake's (1995) terms is both 'intrinsic' and 'instrumental'– that is, it is interesting in its own right, but also illustrates a range of factors involved in policy exchange more generally. Rather like Steiner-Khamsi *et al.* (2006) and Phillips and Ochs (2003), I shall use the term 'policy borrowing' to describe the activities I am discussing here, while recognizing that there is a continuing debate about the appropriateness of that term in relation to possible alternatives. For the moment, I believe it remains the 'least bad' option, although those writers' own use of the complementary concepts of 'policy lending' (Steiner-Khamsi *et al.*, 2006: 217) and 'policy attraction' (Phillips and Ochs, 2003) provide additional insights into the nature of the processes at work.

Against the background of a long tradition of transatlantic policy tourism and policy borrowing from the mid-nineteenth century to the present day, this chapter will consider why the US and England have found each other's education policies so attractive, even in recent years when the educational performance of both countries has been relatively unimpressive in international terms. It will argue that shared assumptive worlds among policymakers are more of an explanation than is evidence that the policies in question actually 'work' on the ground. Indeed, much of the evidence invoked by politicians to justify the borrowing of policies is shown to be highly questionable. However, as we saw in Chapter 1, the questionable use of evidence is also a feature of policy justification at a national level and the growing use of examples of 'what works' elsewhere is a product of the increasing globalization of education policy rather than a distinct phenomenon. So greater emphasis should perhaps now be put upon sharing evidence of 'what doesn't work' to provide a form of 'inoculation' against 'policy epidemics' (Levin, 1998), something that seems particularly relevant in the context of what Sahlberg (2012, 2015) has called GERM, the Global Education 'Reform' Movement.[1]

The tradition of transatlantic policy borrowing

Although policy tourism and policy borrowing have become more common in the context of globalization, they are by no means new. Horace Mann – whose travels to Europe in the 1840s when he was Secretary of the Massachusetts Board of Education are a very early example of education policy tourism – advocated policy borrowing in the following terms:

> I do not hesitate to say that there are many things abroad which we at home should do well to imitate; things some of which are here, as yet, mere matters of speculation and theory, but which, there, have long been in operation, and are now producing a harvest of rich and abundant blessings.
>
> (Mann, 1844: 21)

More recently, in 1995, Ernest L. Boyer, then President of the Carnegie Foundation for the Advancement of Teaching, wrote a foreword for a Carnegie Foundation special report by Kathryn Stearns of the *Washington Post* entitled *School Reform: Lessons from England* (Stearns, 1996). Boyer concluded on the basis of that report that 'there may be some aspects of the British reforms [especially with regard to school choice and school autonomy] that may be worthy of adaptation, if not downright imitation, in the United States'. In the field of school governance in particular, he said, 'England ... might just be the place to turn to learn some important lessons' (Boyer quoted in Stearns, 1996: xviii).

In fact, this was not the first instance of US policy tourists alighting on English school governance reforms as a possible model to emulate at home. In 1991 the Brookings Institution sent John Chubb and Terry Moe to England soon after the publication of their *Politics, Markets and America's Schools* (Chubb and Moe, 1990) to look at school choice and autonomous schools. Their report on the visit, entitled *A Lesson in School Reform from Great Britain* (Chubb and Moe, 1992), concluded:

> In fundamental respects ... Britain is not unique. What is happening there is happening in the United States ... The only real difference is that Britain, owing to its parliamentary form of government, has been able to move farther and faster toward a radical overhaul of its educational system – and is far more likely to succeed. We can only hope it does, and that America can someday follow in Britain's footsteps.
>
> (Chubb and Moe, 1992: 50)

In his introduction to the report, Bruce K. MacLaury, President of the Brookings Institution, commented that 'one would think that the British experience would be receiving careful scrutiny by participants in the emerging American debate. So far, it has not' (Chubb and Moe, 1992: v). However, coming just after the publication of

Stearns's book and Boyer's advice, the education summit of US state governors held in Palisades, New York, in 1996 certainly knew about the English reforms and some of their deliberations were informed by this knowledge. In particular, the expansion of charter schools, and the move to give them increased autonomy in some states, was influenced by the English experience of grant maintained schools that had been allowed by the Thatcher government to opt out of local authority (or school district) control. At that time, there were only 300 charter schools in the US (Nathan, 1996) and they generally had significantly less autonomy than even mainstream schools in England. From that point on they gained wider support, received presidential encouragement and took on forms that now make at least some of them a model for those calling for yet greater freedoms for schools in England.

In the 1990s, the defence of states' rights meant that some of the other English experiments, such as the National Curriculum and a national system of assessment at ages 7, 11, 14 and 16 were likely to be less attractive in the US context, although the developing language of standards and high-stakes testing already showed some similarities to the English approach. Indeed, the then Governor Romer of Colorado actually made reference to the English experience at the National Goals Panel, in connection with America 2000 and Goals 2000 (see Whitty and Edwards, 1998) and, subsequently, No Child Left Behind, the National Governors Association's Common Core Standards and the Obama Administration's Blueprint for Reform have brought the US approach closer to the English one in these areas as well.

Even in the 1990s, there was some traffic in the opposite direction.[2] David Green (1991), in a paper entitled 'Lessons from America' for free-market think tank the Institute of Economic Affairs, commended Chubb and Moe (1990) for the boldness of their arguments in favour of deregulating educational supply and cited Minnesota and East Harlem as successful examples of doing so. From a different point on the political spectrum, David Miliband (1991), then a rising star in what was soon to become New Labour, identified the management of school placements in Cambridge, Massachusetts, as a demonstration of the power of 'controlled parental choice' to reconcile parental preferences with the public goal of 'voluntary' desegregation. In 1990, Her Majesty's Inspectorate of Schools (HMI) went to study teaching and learning in New York City schools (HMI, 1990), while a year earlier they had visited New Jersey to look at 'alternative routes' to teacher training (HMI, 1989). Then, early in this century, Teach for America became the inspiration for the UK's Teach First.

There was even some academic interest in the process of transatlantic policy borrowing at that time, with the Brookings Institution and the University of Warwick hosting a conference to explore the subject, which in turn led to the publication of a collection of papers, entitled *Something Borrowed, Something Learned? The transatlantic market in education and training reform* (Finegold et al., 1993), on both sides of the Atlantic. This work identified 'government ministers, seconded advisers, local government politicians, private sector companies, travelling fellowship programmes and the managers of education institutions' (Finegold *et al.*, 1993: 8) as among the policy tourists implicated in the policy borrowing process.

Nevertheless, despite these precursors in the 1990s, the English interest in US reforms has assumed new proportions in the present century. A keynote speaker at the Conservative Party conference in October 2010 was New York's Geoffrey Canada, who talked about his work at the Harlem Children's Zone, which provided a range of social services to families and children and ran two charter schools at that time. Canada was also one of the stars of Guggenheim's film on the merits of charter schools, *Waiting for 'Superman'* (see Weber, 2010), which was hailed by many in the US, but subjected to a damning critique by Diane Ravitch in *The New York Review of Books* (Ravitch, 2010). It was subsequently promoted by Teach First in the UK.

The following extract from Canada's speech to the Conservative Party neatly illustrates many of the points that will be made in this chapter about policy borrowing and how it works.

> Thank you so much for that warm introduction and good morning everybody.
>
> I was really very excited to come. I actually couldn't wait to come here because there are no two countries that have a closer relationship than the UK and the United States *[applause]* ... and ... I really felt obligated to share with you what we're doing and what we are struggling with. *[Topical joke about the Ryder Cup omitted.]*
>
> When I told my wife I was coming here she said to me 'so Geoff you're friends with President Obama and he's an education reformer' and I said 'that's exactly right'. 'And he's a Democrat', I said 'that's right'.
>
> 'And Mayor Bloomberg in New York City he's an Independent and you're friends with him' and I said 'that's right honey, that's right'.
>
> 'And just last week, you were with the Republican Governor of Newark, Governor Christie, and you say he's your friend also', I said 'that's right honey, that's right'.[3]
>
> She said 'so please explain the Conservative Party to me' *[laughter]*. I said 'well, I hear they're education reformers and if they are I'm going to have a bunch of new friends in the UK'. *[applause]*
>
> Here's why everyone in America is upset with me. I have been making sure our nation knows that we have lost our way. That we have allowed our country – the last remaining superpower on the face of the Earth – to offer

> our children a third world education system *[applause]*. We have failed. We are not in the top ten, in many cases we are not even in the top twenty.
>
> If you look down the road and you say 'what is going on in the US?' you see a nation in decline that is quietly allowing itself to deteriorate because it will not face some tough truths. The fact of the matter is, we have mishandled the education system in our country and now we are at a fork in the road. And I am determined even if the right, the left, the conservatives, the liberals – even if they all are angry at me – I am simply going to tell the truth. If you have a system that is failing your children there is no way that you will remain a great power if you allow your children to get an inferior education *[applause]*.
>
> (Canada, 2010)

In his own speech on this occasion, Michael Gove, the then Conservative Secretary of State for Education, presented charter schools as a model for academy schools and free schools in England, seemingly forgetting that charter schools had themselves been justified by reference to grant maintained schools in England (although he would probably have argued that Labour had reduced their freedoms over the previous 13 years).

Picking up on Canada's comments about common themes in the education policies of opposing political parties, Gove also spoke positively about the policies of President Obama:

> In America, President Obama is pressing ahead with radical school reform to close the gap between rich and poor ...
>
> He is promoting greater autonomy by providing cash and other incentives to encourage more charter schools, the equivalent of our free schools and academies.
>
> He has offered extra support to programmes designed to attract more great people into teaching and leadership.
>
> And he has encouraged states and school districts to provide greater accountability through improved testing and assessment.
>
> (Gove, 2010)

In November 2010, US Education Secretary Arne Duncan was invited by Michael Gove to a breakfast meeting with key English education stakeholders, including sceptical union leaders, to persuade them that charter schools (i.e. academies and free schools in England) were the way to go. During Duncan's visit, the UK Government announced the establishment of its Education Endowment Fund to which groups could bid with ideas about how to turn round under-performing schools. Gove explicitly compared this fund with Barack Obama's Race to the Top initiative, under which states compete for federal cash, saying:

> America is a bigger country and there are differences between us, but I have been impressed by what Race to the Top has done, and impressed by many of the things that President Obama and Arne Duncan have been fighting for.
>
> (Gove, quoted in Vasagar, 2010)

In January 2011, Gove invited Mike Feinberg from the Knowledge is Power Programme (KIPP), one of the most successful chains of charter schools in America, and Joel Klein, former New York City Schools Chancellor, to address a major conference in London to promote free schools. Even at the Labour Party conference in September 2010, there were positive references to the US experience, especially KIPP schools, which Labour politicians had visited during that summer.

It seems, then, that neo-liberal and neo-conservative ideas on education policy are not partisan in a narrow party political sense. In England, there has been considerable continuity at least in direction of travel between Conservative, New Labour and Coalition education policies, while the same is often true of Democrat and Republican policies in the US. Nor is policy borrowing carried out along entirely predictable lines. Democrat administrations in the US have borrowed from Conservative governments in Britain and vice versa. The Conservative Government elected in England in 2015 continues its policy of support for free schools, inspired by charter schools in the US and free schools in Sweden.

Why policy convergence between the UK and the US?

I was already trying to make sense of this in some work undertaken in the 1990s. It began with a paper I gave with Tony Edwards to the American Educational Research Association annual meeting in 1992, which was based partly on my own policy tourism in the US, aided by policy entrepreneur Bruce Cooper of Fordham University, who managed to get onto my itinerary visits that I would not easily have arranged myself, including one to the White House under President George Bush senior.

The paper was substantially revised for publication in *Comparative Education* in 1998, and examined the reasons for policy borrowing between the US and the UK in the field of school choice (Whitty and Edwards, 1998). It explored two different approaches to explaining the apparent convergence of policy. On the one hand, there was evidence of direct policy exchange between the two countries through shared policy networks, some of which are reflected in the examples given above. In other cases, similar policies – or at least similar *sounding* policies – could be identified but without there being any evidence of knowledge on the part of the alleged borrower. We suggested that, superficially at least, there were parallels between the assisted places scheme in England and the Milwaukee choice experiment, which also subsidized access to private education for 'poor' children (Witte, 1993); between local management of schools and site-based management; and between England's city technology colleges and the New American Schools Initiative.

We therefore wondered whether there was a policy zeitgeist associated with post-modernity that could be invoked to explain such similarities in the absence of direct linkages in advance of the policies emerging in both places. Stephen Ball, the journal's guest editor on that occasion, summarized our conclusions as follows:

> Whitty and Edwards ... argue that proposals and justifications for reform in one country provide resources for advocates and politicians interested in promoting change in others. This is not so much a matter of policy exchange but the reinforcement of shared assumptive worlds.
> (Ball, 1998: 119)

This process made use of mutually reinforcing versions of reality that reflected shared assumptions and shared reference groups.[4] We were made aware of some personal links between US policymakers and officials and their British equivalents, through family ties and common educational experiences. These are typical of networks of influence and they reinforced the tendency for the US to look to England (rather than, say, Japan or Germany) in discussions of how best to improve national performance, even though those and other countries were performing better educationally at that time. To that extent, broad political affinity and similar ideological preferences seemed to take precedence even over a concerted search for more effective policies. One Bush government staffer remarked:

> Whereas you heard more about Japan about five years ago, I think you're hearing more people look at England, not Germany so much now. Since the issue is standards and choice, you hear more people talking about England and you guys have done more on the role of unions and things.
> (Whitty and Edwards, 1998: 223)

While economic and social changes put education reform high on the political agenda in both nations, the similarity of response and the interest in sharing New Right ideas derived from a distinctively neo-liberal faith that 'choice and competition' was indeed the answer. In that sense Phillips and Ochs's (2003: 454–5) 'theoretical' basis for deciding what overseas policies were attractive was very much in evidence, albeit alongside examples that also fitted their 'phoney', 'realistic/practical' and 'quick fix' reasons for borrowing.

Although we did not refer to it at the time, our analysis had something in common with Paul Sabatier's Advocacy Coalition Framework (Sabatier and Jenkins-Smith, 1993; Sabatier and Weible, 2007). Our paper was also an example of what Gita Steiner-Khamsi et al. (2006), drawing on the work of Jurgen Schriewer (1990), call an analytical rather than a normative approach to the study of policy borrowing. The same is true of this chapter, at least until towards the end.

Steiner-Khamsi *et al.* (2006) themselves have written cogently about the reasons for policy borrowing, particularly between rich and poor countries in the context of international aid. However, one of the things that is superficially puzzling is why there has been a continuing US–UK nexus in education policy reform that has extended well beyond the close political ties of the Reagan–Thatcher years. It has not apparently been linked to aid, nor is it an obvious example of so-called 'PISA tourism'.

The rise of the importance of PISA (OECD's Programme for International Student Assessment) in education policy discourse has certainly been significant over the last ten years. PISA results (and similar international comparisons) have become 'an event that no-one can afford to miss – it requires answers and demands action' (Grek, 2008). Even in the US, the pressures of globalization and the need for a competitive American workforce have meant that OECD data has fed into President Obama's rhetoric. For example, in his introduction to the *Blueprint for Reform*, reference was made to 'world-class' education in these terms:

> Today more than ever, a world-class education is a pre-requisite for success. America was once the best educated nation in the world. A generation ago, we led all nations in college completion, but today, 10 countries have passed us.
>
> (Obama, 2010: 1)

One impact of international surveys such as PISA has been a focus on education systems that have topped the league tables. There has been increased interest in systems that are shown by PISA results to be succeeding, often on both 'excellence' (high attainment overall) and 'equity' (low influence of socio-economic background on attainment) measures. Finland has, until recently, been the well-known star of the show in this respect (Sahlberg, 2011), so it is not surprising that policymakers there have had to limit the numbers of foreign delegations they can receive as politicians search for the magic bullet. Other countries, and provinces such as Ontario in Canada, have also been the focus of much policy tourism although, following the more recent rounds of PISA, Shanghai-China has become the new destination of choice for education policy tourists, not least among British Government ministers and officials seeking to improve mathematics teaching.[5]

However, PISA *et al.* do not really provide an explanation for the flow of traffic between the UK and the US. Both countries continue to perform embarrassingly badly in many of these tables, so it cannot be that their performance to date justifies the interest they take in each other's reforms. It may be, of course, that the interest in each other's policies is driven by the fact that they are more similar to each other socially and economically than they are to Finland or China. An explanation could thus be that their reforms are more likely to work in each other's countries than the Finnish ones, because the contexts are more similar.[6] Yet the continuing mutual interest in each other's reforms probably remains as much to do with those shared assumptive worlds described above, and, of course, with the existence of a common language in which to describe their reforms.

Dominant discourses of reform

It is, however, possible to overestimate the extent to which similar terms – or even similar substantive policies – are necessary to make reference to other countries' reforms attractive to governments. As already mentioned, there are some clear parallels between grant maintained schools in England and charter schools in the US, and now between charter schools in the US and free schools and academies in England. In these cases the names are different but the content similar. Steiner-Khamsi *et al.* (2006) argue that, conversely, the language of reform may sometimes be the same but the actual content different. Even between the US and the UK, there are cases where the language is similar but the content is significantly, though not entirely, different: No Child Left Behind and Every Child Matters would be one example. Race to the Top and Aimhigher would be another. In both these cases, any cross-referencing would indicate a shared ambition rather than a shared policy prescription.

Steiner-Khamsi *et al.* (2006) also argue that policy borrowing, or rather, reference to practice elsewhere, takes place even when similar reforms already exist in the local context (Steiner-Khamsi and Quist, 2000). This points to the conclusion that it is the discursive and legitimatory work that other people's reforms do for one's own that is important, rather than that they are necessarily new ideas or whether they would actually work in your own context.

Yet this is not how it is often made to appear. One phrase that percolates through much of the education system at both macro-policy level and at classroom level in both countries is 'what works', and this also applies to the discourse of policy borrowing. We are encouraged to learn 'what works' from other countries. Sometimes, this reflects what Phillips and Ochs (2003) describe as 'realistic/practical' reasons for borrowing, although sometimes it is more of a search for their 'quick fix'.

Superficially, an international policy interest in 'what works' should be good news for those who work in research-intensive university schools of education. However, as we noted in Chapter 1, much of the evidence produced by politicians in support of so-called 'evidence-informed' policy is not what university-based researchers would recognize as research. Often it is *quasi*-research carried out by think tanks and advocacy groups.

Observers often do not distinguish between different types of research and the distinctive missions of different types of institutes and foundations.[7] In the context of international policy borrowing, this may be even more of an issue than at home. In the UK, for example, most politicians would know that the Institute of Economic Affairs or the Centre for Policy Studies were neo-liberal think tanks and very different from, say, the Nuffield Foundation. They would not necessarily know that the Manhattan Institute or the Bradley Foundation in the US were very different from the Spencer Foundation. Nor would they realize that, in Canada, the Hudson Institute was a different type of operation from the Ontario Institute for Studies in Education. North American politicians would probably be similarly confused by the UK examples.

Media stories carry details of research but rarely distinguish between different types of research and their varying degrees of robustness. Media reports themselves become the sources of evidence for policy in their own right. There are also crossovers between these various types of evidence. Chubb and Moe undertook their policy tourism as a commission from *The Sunday Times* and, about the same time, *The New York Times* sent Susan Chira, its then education correspondent, on the same journey. Interestingly, Chira made more use of academic research findings in her reports than did Chubb and Moe and, possibly because of this, she produced a more nuanced verdict on the English reforms. But one of the features of media reporting, and herein perhaps lies its appeal to politicians and advocacy groups, is that it tends not to distinguish between anecdote and peer-reviewed research findings when weighing up evidence.

The following example relates to the earlier discussion of the way in which the current government in England is using US charter schools to justify its own policy of freeing up the system by creating academies and free schools outside the control of local authorities. This use of anecdote comes from policy tourism on the part of the person who at that time ran the New Schools Network, a charity that has been engaged by the government to promote free schools and that models itself partly on the New York City Charter School Center. This particular account comes from *The Sunday Times* on 21 February 2010:

> Wolf says her inspiration to set up the New Schools Network, which will act as a 'back-room operation', providing administration and advice, came from a trip to New York. She flew there after working as a researcher for Michael Gove, the Conservative party's education spokesman. The party has championed the new movement, promising ... to permit as many as 3,000 [new free] schools, which are modelled on Sweden's 'free schools' and America's charter movement ...
>
> 'I was reasonably convinced the new schools the Tories were talking about would work. But I wanted to see for myself,' says Wolf.
>
> In New York she saw the contrast between dysfunctional public schools and some of the disciplined, creative charter schools. Sometimes both types of school were housed in one block. 'On one floor of a building I visited, a

girl was being told to put on her hat. I watched her fling it at the staff,' says Wolf. 'When the lift doors opened on the floor of the charter school, by contrast, an 11-year-old came over and asked, ever so politely, would I like to be escorted around.

'I came back to Britain and decided this was what I wanted to do,' she continues. 'I can't think of any other idea that excites me so much.'

(Griffiths, 2010)

Nevertheless, despite the use of such anecdotes in policy borrowing, appeals to the findings of mainstream education research also feature as a key element of policy legitimation. Indeed, in a posting on *The Guardian* website, Wolf herself cited research from Sweden, the US and Alberta, Canada, as evidence that 'new schools perform better, that they have a positive effect on neighbouring schools and that the poorest benefit most' (Wolf, 2010). However, a review of research on Swedish free schools presented a much more nuanced picture (Allen, 2010), while doubts were also raised about the link claimed by Wolf (and by then Secretary of State Gove) between school autonomy and the high levels of educational attainment in Alberta (Evans, 2011).

In another example of the selective use of research, almost as soon as the Coalition Government had been elected in Britain in May 2010 and announced its policies, a document appeared on the website of the UK Department of Education, entitled 'Mythbuster'.[8] It included, along with selective use of UK and Swedish research findings, the following references to research on US charter schools:

The Case for School Freedom: National and International Evidence

Free Schools Raise Standards
- A recent study concluded that Boston's charter schools 'have a consistently positive impact on student achievement.' ...
- New York has instituted a 'report card' system ... The charter schools have performed better than other schools, with the majority received (*sic*) As and Bs ...
- Recent studies from Chicago and Florida indicate that charter school students have higher ACT scores, higher graduation rates and a greater probability of attending college than students who attend traditional public schools ...

Free Schools Help the Disadvantaged
- Charter schools in New York have been shown to dramatically close the gap separating inner-city neighbourhood students from those of the wealthiest suburbs ...
- The Harlem Children's Zone charters have completely closed the black–white achievement gap at both elementary and middle school level ...

- Charter schools in Chicago close half of the achievement gap between disadvantaged inner-city public school students and middle-income students in suburban districts ...

Debunking Myths About School Freedom

Myth: Free Schools will only benefit the well-off

Reality:

91 percent of New York charter school students participate in the Free or Reduced-Price lunch program (compared with 72 percent of students in the traditional state schools) ...

Myth: Free Schools will covertly select the most able pupils

Reality:

The major report on Chicago charter schools found that the charters studied drew students who were, on average, lower achieving than public school students in the neighbourhoods where the schools were located.

(Extracted from 'Mythbuster', Department for Education website, 2010; has been subsequently removed)

This document was sent to some US researchers to gauge their reactions, and the following response was typical of the comments received:

> Most of what they are claiming is technically true, but quite skewed in selection and interpretation. They only select from the minority of studies – like the study of New York City – that support their claims. Some of those localities indeed have some very good charter schools. However, *Mythbuster* ignores the many larger and more representative studies, like the recent national study out of Stanford [CREDO], that show charter schools, on average, underperforming compared to other public schools. I don't think that any of the studies they cite were peer-reviewed, and almost all were done by charter advocates.
>
> They are not only selective in choosing studies, but make claims from those studies without including the usual caveats and cautions. For instance, the claims about higher test scores – while technically correct – show no indication that the authors are aware that charter schools often exclude more difficult to educate students. The tenuous assertion that charter schools do not select more able students is drawn from a 2005 magazine article, which was in fact based on 3 schools in one city. There are a number of peer-reviewed studies that show the opposite.
>
> (Lubienski, C. (2010), personal communication, 22 June)

A number of reports from the National Education Policy Center in Boulder, Colorado, have also cast doubt on some dubious assertions made about charter schools in American right-wing think tank reports and subsequently repeated as facts in the UK government's 'Mythbuster' mentioned above.[9]

Policy borrowing or just policymaking on a global scale?

However, this use of research is probably merely an example of the globalization of education policymaking, rather than something that is peculiar to policy *borrowing*. While it may be harder to scrutinize the validity of claims about the impact of policies being implemented elsewhere, there is nothing unusual in the selective use of research findings in policymaking. Indeed, as we saw in Chapter 1, there have been many examples in English policymaking over many years. Ravitch's review of *Waiting for 'Superman'*, entitled 'The Myth of Charter Schools' (Ravitch, 2010), identifies a similar phenomenon in the US. She points out that the Guggenheim film quietly acknowledges that only one in five charter schools achieves 'amazing results', but fails to explore why there are twice as many failing charter schools as there are successful ones, despite the wide availability of the CREDO study from Stanford that showed this. Similar concerns about the use of research evidence have actually been expressed by both sides of the debate about charter schools (Henig, 2008).

More generally, the use of research in claims about 'what works' is particularly interesting. The language of 'what works' has been influential in the US since the 1980s and, as mentioned in Chapter 1, was adopted enthusiastically in the UK as part of Tony Blair's modernization of the Labour Party and its abandonment of supposedly outdated ideologies. It remained a key part of the Coalition Government's discourse in the UK and seems to have been a crucial element of Race to the Top in the US, which President Obama stated would 'not be based on politics, ideology, or the preferences of a particular interest group. Instead, it will be based on a simple principle – whether a state is ready to do "what works"' (quoted in Mathis and Welner, 2010: 2). The *Blueprint* similarly makes reference to prioritizing approaches to reform 'on the strengths of their evidentiary base' (*ibid*).

However, the way in which academic research is actually used as part of that 'evidentiary base' by politicians is disturbing. A publication from the National Education Policy Center by William Mathis and Kevin Welner concludes that criticisms made by Gene Glass of the evidence cited in the 1986 report *What Works* (US Department of Education, 1986) also apply to the six summaries of research issued by the Obama government to support Obama's education *Blueprint for Reform* in 2010. Glass had said of *What Works*:

> The selection of research to legitimize political views is an activity engaged in by governments at every point on the political compass ... *What works* does not synthesize research, it invokes it in a modern ritual seeking

legitimation of the Reagan administration's policies ... and, lest one forget, previous administrations have done the same.

(Glass, 1987: 9).

Mathis and Welner, and the researchers who reviewed the six *Blueprint* reports, suggest that the same is true of the present US administration. They conclude:

> The overall quality of the [research] summaries is far below what is required for a national policy discussion of critical issues. Each of the summaries was found to give overly simplified, biased, and too-brief explanations of complex issues.
>
> (Mathis and Welner, 2010: 3)

None of this should be surprising either in the context of national policy or its use of research evidence from overseas. The contributors to the Mathis and Welner book seem very disappointed to find governments doing this sort of thing. But as Glass pointed out years earlier, that disappointment should be leavened with a cynical expectation that it is par for the course. As we saw in Chapter 1, while researchers may ideally wish policy to be based on robust research findings, in reality policy is driven by all sorts of considerations and the findings of education research will sometimes be rather low down the list. According to Levin (1998), other influences include the vicissitudes of the moment, the requirements of staying in office and the beliefs, commitments and prejudices of policymakers and their advisors and constituents. More fundamentally, we have to acknowledge that politics is significantly shaped by symbolic considerations that may have little to do with the real effects of policies.

This does not excuse blatant misrepresentation of research findings but, as indicated earlier, we are often talking here about a more subtle process of 'elective affinity' where work that falls within policymakers' comfort zone is more likely to be attended to than that that questions the validity of the assumptions with which they operate. This means that they rarely draw on the full range of education research, which in turn may have consequences for funding. While we do need to be realistic about the context in which research is used, it can be particularly frustrating that politicians are often not interested in the more profound questions researchers want to ask. Researchers quite reasonably want to ask questions that go beyond 'what works', and it is often the answers to these questions that explain why 'what works' sometimes does not work. Always important, but especially so in the context of cross-cultural research and policy borrowing, are questions about 'what works where, with whom, and why'.[10] Some research can also have a role in helping people to think about questions such as whether what policymakers are trying to do is worthwhile, and what constitutes socially just schooling, although politicians tend to see that as their job rather than that of education researchers.

For all these reasons and more, achieving consensus on the evidence needed to establish 'what works' and to base education policy on that is unlikely to be an attainable goal, even if such a technicist utopia were desirable. This is not to suggest that there is no role for a 'what works' approach to education research but, as we argued in Chapter 1, the notion that this is the only type of research that should be encouraged or funded certainly needs to be resisted.

On policy borrowing, Andy Hargreaves (2008: 118) rightly suggests that policy principles may travel better than policies and that they are 'much more transposable and transportable if they are interpreted intelligently within communities of practice among and between those who are their bearers and recipients'. But the fact that they may be transposable among communities of political practice in the manner described earlier in this chapter does not ensure that they are transposable to communities of educational practice within which sensitivity to context is crucial to success. And it is this element that is obscured by the sort of political grandstanding described earlier and, in particular, its tendency to disregard the nuances that research properly records.

Conclusion

I have argued in this chapter that there has been a long tradition of transatlantic policy tourism and policy borrowing since the mid-nineteenth century, reflecting shared assumptive worlds among policymakers in Britain and the US. I have also suggested that, in the discourse of policymaking at all levels, questionable use of evidence is often part of policy justification. However, in the context of globalization, there has been an increasing tendency to invoke claims about 'what works' in other countries and I have pointed here to some of the dangers and limitations of this approach.

So what might be the alternative to policy borrowing as it is currently practised? Given the host of initiatives that have been launched and abandoned over the past 30 years, there may be value in a more modest goal of reaching some agreement on 'what doesn't work', even across national contexts. In this connection, Levin (1998) once used the notion of 'policy epidemic' as a tool for thinking about cross-national policy sharing and asked whether the 'prevention' of disease could be a similarly useful idea to apply to inappropriate education policies.

All this provides a somewhat different perspective on cross-national policy sharing and is reminiscent of something else said by Horace Mann about his policy tourism in Europe as Secretary of the Massachusetts Board of Education. As well as leading Mann to advocate 'positive' policy borrowing, his experiences also led him to reflect that:

> if we are wise enough to learn from the experience of others rather than await the infliction consequent upon our own errors, we may yet escape

The (mis)use of evidence in policy borrowing

the magnitude and formidableness of those calamities under which some other communities are now suffering.

(Mann, 1844)

In fact, Edwards and I identified an example of 'negative' policy borrowing in our 1998 paper (Whitty and Edwards, 1998), when we noted that:

> Britain's independent National Commission on Education (1993: 185) cited the Carnegie Foundation's (1992) study of school choice to justify its own warning that similar reforms in England's steeply tiered education system could have the 'unacceptable consequence' of increasingly unequal opportunities.
>
> (Whitty and Edwards, 1998: 214)

In this case, there was a clear recognition both of the possibilities of learning lessons from abroad and of the importance of context. Such an approach would probably not appeal to politicians looking for magic bullets, but it might be more appealing to a wider public who tend, like many researchers, to be sceptical about magic bullets.

Although pointing out the limitations of charter schools, for example, to policymakers can sometimes seem fruitless, education researchers also have a wider job as public intellectuals in addressing broader public attitudes to education policy and reform. Henig (2008) concludes a fascinating, and not entirely depressing, account of how research has been used in US policy debates on charter schools with the encouraging claim that 'shifting the center of gravity of public discourse towards a higher level of sophistication seems within grasp, and seems likely also to generate positive results' (Henig, 2008: 245).

In the UK, the Fabian Society, which in view of my earlier comments I should clearly identify as a left-of-centre think tank, published a report in 2010 on narrowing the attainment gap between students from different socio-economic backgrounds (Bamfield and Horton, 2010). What made this piece of research stand out was its emphasis on the need to address public opinion in relation to educational inequality and counter the way in which this has too often been shaped by misleading political narratives around 'educational failure'.

Education researchers can help in challenging such narratives and changing the terms of the debate by reinforcing messages, not just about what works, but also about what *doesn't* work and why it doesn't work. In Levin's terms, cross-national comparisons of reform may provide a way of strengthening the public mind on education to increase 'resistance' to superficial but seemingly attractive policies.

Policy inoculation may thus be a more appropriate metaphor than policy borrowing, especially in the context of Sahlberg's subsequent coining of the term GERM to describe the sorts of reforms on school choice and school autonomy discussed in this chapter (Sahlberg, 2012). As implied in Chapter 1, such educative work in civil society might in time come to be seen as at least as legitimate a form of impact for education researchers as the questionable 'quick fixes' encouraged by too narrow a 'what works' philosophy. But it should be clear from what has been said in this chapter that, in a globalizing world, this work will now need to take place on a global as well as a national scale.[11]

Notes

[1] Another striking metaphor for this movement that I came across recently is the 'rubber duckies' phenomenon, alluding to a cargo of identical toy ducks that was lost from a container ship and subsequently washed up on beaches all around the world, just as similar education reforms have spread on a global scale (Fischetti, 2014).

[2] There were, of course, earlier examples in that direction as well. Beresford-Hill (1993) cites Board of Education visits to America in 1900 on behalf of Michael Sadler.

[3] Governor Christie was in fact Governor of the state of New Jersey, in which Newark is located.

[4] These are important aspects of what Ball himself would later characterize as 'network governance' (see Ball, 2012; Ball and Junemann, 2012).

[5] See, for example, British Education Minister Elizabeth Truss's mission to Shanghai in 2014, which led to Chinese teachers spending time advising and teaching in English schools (DfE, 2014b).

[6] Jerrim and Vignoles (2015), in the first major evaluation of attempts to introduce East Asian mathematics teaching approaches into English schools, are tentatively positive about their potential impact. However, it is interesting that they report on 'borrowing' from Singapore (rather than Shanghai), where there have been English as well as Chinese cultural influences on education. P. Morris (2015) is sceptical about the possibilities of successful policy exchange between East Asia and England, and, indeed, about policy borrowing more generally. He points to various ways in which complexities are glossed over as overseas evidence is invoked to serve political agendas at home. See also Auld and Morris (2014, forthcoming).

[7] Britain has a much weaker tradition than the US of philanthropic organizations being involved in education research and advocacy, but it is now becoming an increasingly important feature of the UK landscape (Ball, 2009).

[8] It is unclear whether this document was originally intended to be made publicly available, at least in the form it was, as it was not presented to the usual high standards of official documentation. A similar type of document, but one that was more professionally produced (DfE, 2010a), appeared alongside the Coalition Government's 2010 schools White Paper, *The Importance of Teaching* (DfE, 2010b), mentioned in Chapter 2 above.

[9] See http://nepc.colorado.edu/publications.

[10] On this issue, it is somewhat reassuring to learn that, after a period when the US administration seemed to favour a crude 'what works' agenda, the US Institute of Education Sciences has belatedly granted greater priority to putting research findings into context by asking 'how, why, for whom, and under what conditions' policies are effective (National Board for Educational Sciences, 2010).

[11] Of course, when policy borrowing involves West–East, North–South, developed–developing country interchange, additional considerations enter into the picture, such as those mentioned above in relation to Steiner-Khamsi's work. In seeking to understand the ways in which 'British educational reform' has been used in the Japanese education context, Takayama and Apple (2008) point to the need to employ not only the literature of policy borrowing, but also that of postcolonial studies and cultural studies.

Chapter 4

'Closing the achievement gap'
Rhetoric or reality?
with Jake Anders

Introduction

A key focus in English education policy has been on 'narrowing the gap', meaning reducing persistent social class differences in educational achievement, even though the terms 'poverty', 'disadvantage', 'deprivation', or 'social exclusion' are often used in place of overt reference to social class, and these are usually measured in terms of socio-economic status (SES) or eligibility for free school meals (FSM) (Whitty, 2001). For much of the latter half of the last century there were also major concerns about the underachievement of girls. That gender gap has been largely reversed, although not in the hard sciences or at the very highest levels in some other subjects (Ringrose, 2013). Minority ethnic achievement has also been a concern, although there are significant differences in the performance of different minority groups (Gillborn and Mirza, 2000; Alexander *et al.* 2015; Ward, 2015).

The emphasis in this chapter is on gaps between socio-economic groups as identified through cognitive measures and the achievement of academic qualifications. This is not intended to suggest that the only purpose of schooling is to achieve such qualifications, or that those who fail to do so are deficient, either absolutely or relatively, in other important respects. Indeed, under the New Labour Government in the early years of this century there was, for example, considerable emphasis on the role of education in fostering 'well-being'. One difficulty in establishing the impact of other aspects of education, however, is that data in these areas are limited and highly contentious. Furthermore, in the present political climate in England, many of those advocating the importance of these wider aspects of education find themselves justifying them in terms of their impact on attainment (see, for example, Harrison *et al.*, 2015). Although this may seem to be ceding too much in the argument over the purposes of education, there is a great deal of evidence that life chances in English society are closely linked to school attainment in a myriad of ways and that personal fulfilment and social justice could both be enhanced by narrowing or closing long-standing academic achievement and participation gaps (Schuller *et al.*, 2004). As Kerr and West (2010: 16) put it, 'despite the dangers of narrowing our view of what education is about', a focus on attainment is justifiable because 'attainment undeniably has important consequences for life chances'.

Geoff Whitty with Jake Anders

One specific reason why it is important to address the academic attainment gap in schools is that student performance during the compulsory phase of education has significant implications for access to higher education and the labour market. As discussed in the next chapter, there has been a considerable and, at least until recently, persistent gap in England in the rates of participation in higher education between different social groups and in their opportunities for access to employment in science and technology and the professions (Kelly and Cook, 2007). There has also been a strong tendency for students at elite universities to be drawn from more affluent families (Boliver, 2011). Yet, as we shall see in Chapter 5, although there may still be some financial and aspirational barriers to widening participation and ensuring fair access in higher education, it is clear that one of the major impediments to pupils proceeding to university is low prior attainment.

The present chapter will concentrate on attempts to narrow the gap in the compulsory phase of schooling (ages 5–16), as well as identifying the sorts of interventions in those years that the evidence suggests may have some potential to break the enduring link between social background and educational achievement. It is important to note, however, that parallel policies have been pursued in relation to pre-school (NESS, 2010) and post-compulsory education (Harris, 2010).

(How) did New Labour narrow the attainment gap in English schools, 1997–2010?

The New Labour Government elected in 1997 under the leadership of Tony Blair increasingly made narrowing the attainment gap between children from different socio-economic backgrounds a key part of its educational policy (Lupton and Obolenskaya, 2013). Given this goal, it is perhaps surprising that data on the trends for this gap are somewhat patchy. While there are figures on the gap at particular points in time, they often use different measures of attainment and/or different comparator groups, making the assessment of trends quite difficult. It is also the case that, in the initial period of New Labour Government, apart from Education Action Zones (EAZs) (an ill-fated initiative that put modest extra resources into areas of multiple deprivation), the major emphasis was on driving up standards overall. It was only the failure of this approach to impact significantly on social differences in attainment that led to specific policies after 2001 to address the attainment gap, with a major thrust in this direction after 2005. Although there were increases in average levels of attainment in the first period of the New Labour Government, some have argued that even these increases were at least partly achieved through grade inflation (Tymms, 2004). Evidence of the gap narrowing is similarly open to different interpretations.

Figure 4.1 shows trends in the attainment gap up until 2003, and suggests a slight narrowing of the gap between pupils from non-manual and manual families.

'Closing the achievement gap'

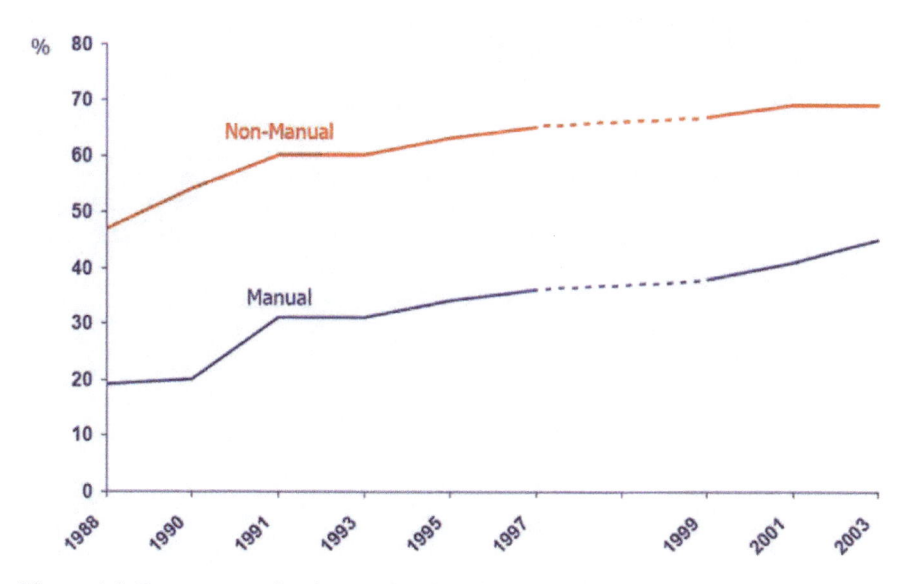

Figure 4.1: Percentage of cohort achieving 5+ A*–C GCSEs by parents' social class (1988–2003)

Note: Discontinuity exists from 1997 to 1999 because of a change in the classification of social class from socio-economic group (SEG) to National Statistics Socio-economic Classification (NSSEC). Manual and non-manual categories have been constructed by grouping more detailed breakdowns of social class groups. The 'other' group has been excluded from the analysis.

Source: DfES (2006) analysis of Youth Cohort Study cohorts 4–12, sweep 1.

The Office for National Statistics (ONS, 2006) provides data on changes in the attainment gap from 2002 and 2005. These figures show a reduction in the attainment gap between pupils eligible for FSM and those ineligible for FSM in terms of the proportions obtaining no passes in the General Certificate of Secondary Education (GCSEs) (or equivalents) and those obtaining five or more A*–C GCSEs (or equivalents). These figures show a stronger trend towards narrowing when IDACI (an area-based indicator of deprivation) is used instead of FSM eligibility. This is because this measure compares the most deprived with the least deprived, rather than the most deprived with the rest, and there seems to be evidence of generalized catching up between the bottom three deprivation quartiles and the top. In the FSM measures this catching up by pupils in the middle reduced the relative gains of the bottom compared to the top.

Cook (2011) presents evidence, summarized in Figure 4.2, of a further reduction in the attainment gap between 2006 and 2010. He uses performance relative to the mean in sciences, modern languages, maths, English, history and geography, generally regarded as the core subjects. In this case the size of the reduction looks to be relatively modest and concentrated among those in the bottom fifth of households as ranked by deprivation.

57

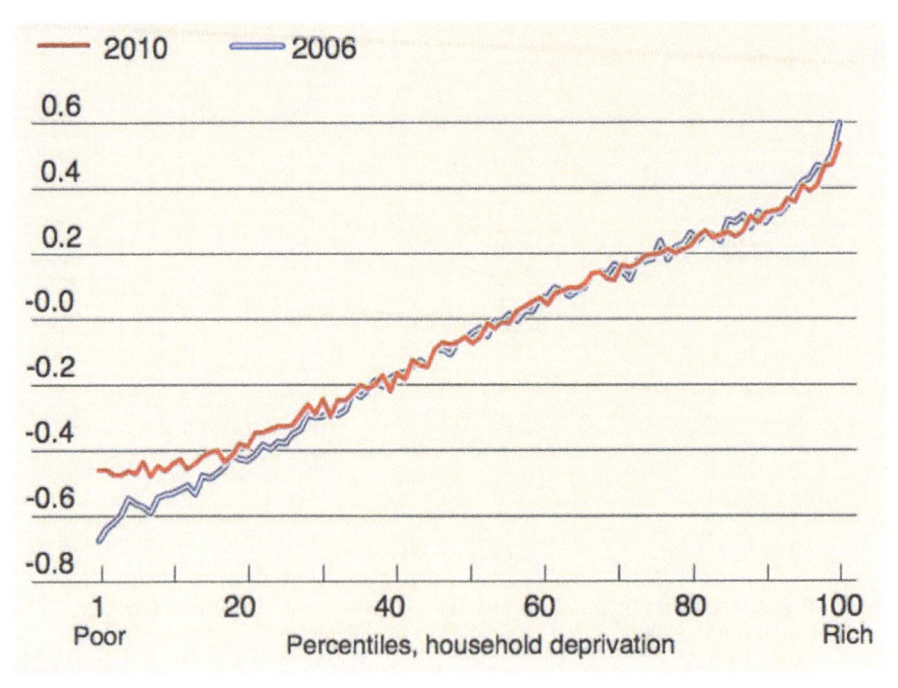

Figure 4.2: Graph showing relation between household deprivation and relative performance in GCSE point score in core subjects

Note: Vertical axis shows standard deviation from mean GCSE point-score performance in the core subjects of sciences, modern languages, maths, English, history and geography. Percentiles of household deprivation derived using Income Deprivation Affecting Children Index (IDACI).

Source: Cook's (2011) analysis of National Pupil Database.

This analysis shows a steady weakening of the overall correlation between the two factors in the years between 2006 and 2010. Interestingly, this is the case particularly for KS4 attainment overall, where performance on some vocational courses is included. It could be argued that this lends some support to the charge that part of the decline in the socio-economic attainment gap is due to lower-performing pupils being diverted to alternative courses (de Waal, 2008). However, as the core measure still shows a decline, not all of the reduction in the gap can be dismissed as illusory, even if one were to accept the argument that the alternative courses are somehow less rigorous or marketable.

Although by most measures there was thus a small reduction in the attainment gap under the New Labour Government of 1997–2010, it must be regarded as a disappointing achievement when compared with the aspirations of successive prime ministers and secretaries of state for education. Not surprisingly, the Coalition Government that took over in 2010 tended to dismiss even the limited narrowing of the gap that was achieved under New Labour, regarding it as a poor return on the significant amount of public resources invested. This picture is summarized and

'Closing the achievement gap'

restated in the Coalition Government's Social Mobility Strategy (HM Government, 2010b), and presented graphically in Figure 4.3 under the government's original, politically loaded heading.

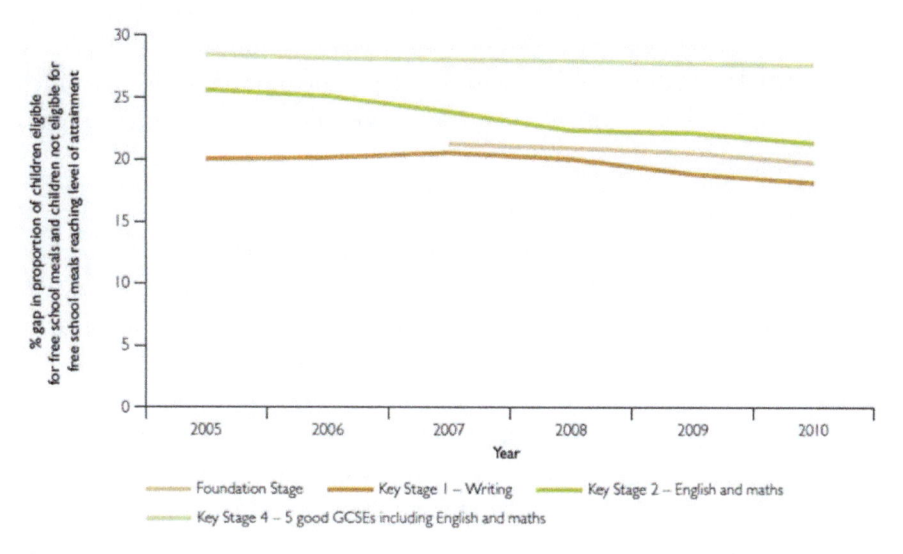

Figure 4.3: Gaps in educational performance have narrowed only very slightly despite significant investment
Source: HM Government (2010b: 20), drawing on data from various sources.

What may have contributed to the narrowing of the gap?

There were considerable numbers of educational initiatives during the period of the New Labour Government, reflecting a variety of different understandings about how best to close the gap. They ranged from area-based interventions like the aforementioned Education Action Zones, Excellence in Cities, and the London Challenge, through large-scale nationwide interventions like the National Strategies for Literacy and Numeracy, the introduction of 'floor targets' for all schools, a remodelling of the school workforce, including the use of more teaching assistants, improving school leadership training, enhancing teacher quality, the creation of a network of specialist schools and the foundation of academy schools outside the local authority system, to the 'personalization' of education through individually targeted interventions such as Reading Recovery. In addition, there was Every Child Matters, a multi-agency policy that addressed a wider 'children's agenda' and placed a particular emphasis on the safety and well-being of children and young people.

The vast numbers of education policies introduced by New Labour led to charges of 'initiative-itis', while the tendency to alter them even before they had been properly evaluated has meant that it is virtually impossible to determine across the system as a whole which policies were effective in narrowing the gap. This is despite the fact that, as described in Chapter 1, the government espoused an 'evidence-based' approach to policy and often employed the rhetoric of 'what works' (see Ofsted, 2010b).

For some policies, specifically Education Action Zones, Excellence in Cities and the employment of teaching assistants, the evidence is equivocal or suggests little or even negative impact (Power *et al.*, 2004; Machin *et al.*, 2007; Blatchford *et al.*, 2012). We shall therefore focus here on some of the policies for which there does seem to be some credible evidence that they did make a positive impact on the attainment gap.

The National Strategies

The National Strategies for Literacy (from September 1998) and Numeracy (from September 1999) were a key early policy enacted by Labour to attempt to raise standards overall. An evaluation of a major plank of the National Strategy for Literacy, namely the 'literacy hour', was conducted by Machin and McNally at the London School of Economics. This identified a significant impact for the literacy hour in its piloted form as part of the earlier National Literacy Programme (NLP). It found that 'reading and English Key Stage 2 levels rose by more in NLP schools between 1996 and 1998' than in the comparator schools that had not yet introduced the policy (Machin and McNally, 2004: 27).

A more critical view has been taken by a series of reports by Tymms and colleagues (Tymms, 2004; Tymms *et al.*, 2005; Tymms and Merrell, 2007). These question the extent to which standards have truly increased, by using secondary data on pupil performance that are argued to be more comparable over time. While it does seem likely that some of the increase in apparent performance has been due to grade inflation it should not detract from quasi-experimental evidence, such as that used by Machin and McNally, since there is no particular reason to think inflation would affect the pilot schools more than comparator schools.

However, the results found by Machin and McNally relate to very early impacts of the intervention. It seems plausible that parts of these effects are due simply to the increased focus generated by the introduction of these strategies. Indeed, the evaluation of the National Literacy and Numeracy Strategies commissioned by the DfES suggests that 'the initial gains in the 1999 national tests were likely due largely to higher motivation on the part of teachers and others at the local level' (Earl *et al.*, 2001: 5). This would also explain the tailing off in improvements observed in general performance over the period.

More generally Earl *et al.* (2001) were positive about the Strategies' impact in terms of implementation, suggesting they brought about large shifts in priorities within almost all schools in the country. They describe the Strategies as 'successful' at more than one point in their report. However, in a critique similar to that later developed by Tymms, Goldstein (2002) suggests the report relied too much on test performance at KS2 to justify extrapolating from successful implementation to success in raising standards.

Machin and McNally (2004) also noted particularly strong effects at lower levels of attainment (but still positive effects for those already achieving above the target level) and an increased impact for boys (who were otherwise lagging) compared to girls. The results on differential impacts at varying levels of ability fit well with the suggestion by Jerrim (2012) of a reduction in the attainment gap at the bottom of the ability distribution, and suggest that the Strategies may have been more effective in this respect than their critics claim.

Evaluation of the National Strategies is a difficult task for several reasons. Elements such as the Literacy and Numeracy Strategies were rolled out rapidly and comprehensively, quickly becoming a pervasive part of the education system. The Strategies also had many elements, reaching across early years, primary, secondary, behaviour and attendance, and school improvement programmes. Many evaluations point only to overall improvements in attainment over the period (DfE, 2011), implicitly treating almost all New Labour education policies as part of the National Strategies. They also tend to provide only descriptive evidence, and we have no indication of what would have happened in the presence of different policies, or a continuation of previous policies. Indeed, the inspectorate for schools (Ofsted) has pointed to the failure to evaluate which elements of the National Strategies were successful as a serious shortcoming stemming partly from the sheer number of initiatives introduced in a relatively short period of time. Its report does, however, praise the impact that the National Strategies have had on increased debate around pedagogy, suggesting almost all schools feel they have led to an improvement in teaching and learning and the use of assessment (Ofsted, 2010b: 5).

Specific evaluation of the 'Narrowing the Gaps' element of the National Strategies was carried out by York Consulting (Starks, 2011). This focused on support and resources both for children eligible for FSM and for Gypsy, Roma and Traveller (GRT) children. It describes finding evidence of increased use of the practices that their literature review suggests are effective in improving pupil attendance, motivation, confidence and attainment. These included capacity building by local authorities to support schools in achieving goals, improved engagement with parents and intelligent tracking of pupil attainment. For the reasons referred to above, there is little specific quantitative evidence of how this feeds through into outcomes beyond the national trends in attainment gaps identified earlier. The limited case study evidence on the reduction of gaps is not particularly encouraging, with only three out of the eight case-study schools reducing the attainment gap. However, it is not clear how representative these case studies were, and the conclusion appears to relate to a rather limited time frame (although it is not entirely clear exactly what this is). The report suggests that the Strategies were anyway not fully implemented by the end of the period and it argues that with continued support we may see further positive results.

Ultimately, the National Strategies seem to have had a limited impact on the attainment gap, while their overall impact plateaued in later years. By then, and well before it lost the 2010 election, the New Labour Government had decided that such large-scale national initiatives were no longer appropriate. Its Children's Plan envisaged much greater local and professional autonomy in driving improvement in the future (DCSF, 2007). This was consistent with a wider trend towards handing more responsibility to schools and federations of schools, including autonomous academies and chains of such academies (Curtis, 2009).

Academies

Academies were based on an expectation that giving greater autonomy to schools with dynamic leadership teams and private sponsorship would improve their performance. Some of these academies were new schools in disadvantaged areas, while others were existing schools deemed to be failing under local authority supervision. An official evaluation conducted by PricewaterhouseCoopers on behalf of the DfES (PWC, 2008) notes an increased level of performance in these schools relative to the national average. However, this methodology has been criticized (Machin and Vernoit, 2011) on two main counts. First, new academies during the period of evaluation had a significantly more disadvantaged intake relative to the national average. Second, changes in the socio-economic status of the intake frequently accompanied the opening of an academy, and these have the potential to further undermine the validity of the comparison.

An evaluation by the National Audit Office (NAO) used a more select group of comparator schools, based on their intake and performance relative to the academies prior to conversion. This found increases in performance, but the analysis suggests this was largely driven by the 'substantial improvements by the less disadvantaged pupils' (NAO, 2007: 27). While improvements are of course to be welcomed, this does not seem particularly promising for reducing attainment gaps between pupils from differing socio-economic backgrounds unless there are substantial peer effects. On the other hand, as Maden (2002: 336) once put it, successful schools tend to have 'a "critical mass" of more engaged, broadly "pro-school" children to start with', so a longer term perspective may be helpful here.

In their own study, Machin and Vernoit (2011) went further to try to overcome the potential for selection bias in the choice of comparator schools. They used maintained schools that went on to become academies after their data collection period. Their analysis yielded preliminary results suggesting that in the academies an extra three percentage points of pupils achieved top grades (5 A*–C) at GCSE (or equivalents). However, they identified this effect only in academies that had been open for more than two years at the time of their evaluation. Interestingly, their results suggested that despite the same increase in the socio-economic status of the school's intake noted above (and the consequent reduction for neighbouring schools) there were also increases in performance in those neighbouring schools, perhaps due to increased competition. This finding runs counter to the claims made by most critics of academies, who regard their success as coming at the expense of other local schools.

Further work by Machin and colleagues delved into the ways in which academies achieved improvements in their own outcomes. Their findings are not encouraging for proponents of the policy as a way of closing gaps in performance: they suggest that in general those academies that converted between 2002 and 2007 improved their results by 'further raising the attainments of pupils in the top half of the ability distribution, and in particular pupils in the top 20% tail' (Machin and Silva, 2013: 2) and not by improving the results of those in the bottom tail. In addition, they found no evidence of improvements among the academies converting in 2008 and 2009. Perhaps this suggests that conversion to academies is a useful policy only in certain circumstances. Unfortunately, the incoming Coalition Government cancelled an evaluation of academies commissioned by the previous government, which may have shed further light on these issues.

There is no doubt that some of the academies founded under New Labour proved successful in improving the attainment of disadvantaged pupils. However, not all academies have performed so well in this, and indeed other, respects. As Curtis *et al.* (2008) argued, 'Academies are in danger of being regarded by politicians as a panacea for a broad range of education problems'. They pointed out that, given the variable performance of academies to date, 'conversion to an Academy may not always be the best route to improvement' and that care needed to be taken 'to ensure they are the "best fit" solution to the problem at hand' (Curtis *et al.*, 2008: 10). A recent House of Commons Select Committee report raised doubts about the evidence that academization drives improvement, although it was more positive about the impact of the early New Labour academies than those created under the current government (House of Commons, 2015). A further analysis by Eyles and Machin (2015) has confirmed that the first round of academy conversions that took place in the 2000s generated significant improvements in pupil performance, but also that the extent of improvement varied according to the prior characteristics of the school and that changes in head teachers and management structures were the key factors in improvements in pupil outcomes.

Extended Schools

Extended schools and full-service extended schools (similar to full-service schools or 'wrap-around schooling' in the USA) were introduced to provide an extended day and/or additional services on school sites. The evaluation of New Labour's pilot programme of full-service extended schools found that the number of pupils reaching the national benchmark at age 16 (five good GCSEs) in such schools rose faster than the national average, and that it brought particularly positive outcomes for poorer families by providing stability and improving their children's engagement in learning. Encouragingly in terms of the concerns of this paper, the final report indicated that the achievement gap between advantaged and disadvantaged pupils, based on FSM eligibility, had narrowed in these schools (Cummings *et al.*, 2007: 126).

Reading Recovery

Support for Reading Recovery was an example of a policy targeted directly at individuals rather than schools or areas, and was part of a broader personalization agenda that developed in the later years of the New Labour administration. Reading Recovery originated in New Zealand but was introduced in England by the IOE; given some government funding, it eventually became a key component of the national Every Child a Reader programme.[4] It provides one-on-one support to children falling behind their peers in the first few years of school, and thus to break the cycle of low self-esteem and lack of confidence that results from falling behind and hampers further progress. A Reading Recovery evaluation (NatCen, 2011) saw statistically significant improvements in reading ability and reading-related attitudes and behaviours for children receiving help from the programme. It is worth noting, however, that this is a purely descriptive analysis; no comparator group can be identified, since pupils who should receive the Reading Recovery are only selected in schools where it is being implemented. As such, we cannot say what progress these children would have made in the absence of Reading Recovery. It could be the case that some would have caught up by themselves or through pre-existing support mechanisms, or alternatively that they would have fallen further behind. The same evaluation also used a quasi-experimental method to estimate the wider impact of Every Child a Reader. This found an encouraging impact on reading and writing attainment of between two and six percentage points in the later years of the intervention.

Teach First

There has been an increasing recognition 'that getting the right people to become teachers is critical to high performance' (Barber and Mourshed, 2007: 16). Teach First, like Teach for America, was an initiative to recruit highly qualified graduates into teaching in particularly disadvantaged schools. It began work in London in 2002. An evaluation by Muijs *et al.* (2010) provides indicative results that schools with Teach First teachers achieve higher attainment for their pupils than comparable schools (as matched by type of school, gender intake, performance levels, student intake characteristics, location and school size). As with any quasi-experimental method we cannot be sure that the results are causal, since the matching will not be able to ensure the schools are truly comparable; indeed, since schools choose if they wish to partner with Teach First there seems considerable scope for those with more proactive leadership or more capacity to benefit from Teach First teachers to be driving these results. The evaluation attempts to assess this possibility by also comparing Ofsted evaluations of Teach First and comparator schools, finding little significant difference. It also finds some evidence of a mild, but significant, correlation between the number of Teach First teachers in a school and its student outcomes, a pattern we would expect where such teachers are making a real difference to the pupils' attainment. While this does not give us specific evidence on closing the attainment gap, since all Teach First schools have disadvantaged intakes, it seems plausible that this initiative can help to reduce school attainment gaps.

London Challenge

The transformation of schooling in London under New Labour is worthy of particular attention. Wyness (2011) notes that, while the demographic character of London would lead one to expect that educational outcomes in London would be inferior to those in the rest of the country, London pupils actually perform better than those in the rest of the country at most ages and levels of attainment. Performing similarly well to the rest of the country at KS1, London pupils 'pull away from their non-London counterparts at Key Stage 2, with the gap remaining constant, or increasing at Key Stage 4' (Wyness, 2011: 47). It has even been claimed that, for reasons we explore below, London is the only capital city in the developed world whose schools perform better than those in the rest of their nations (Stewart, 2011).

One of the possible explanations Wyness offers for this is London Challenge, a policy introduced in 2003 at a time when there was something of a 'moral panic' about the performance of London's schools. The policy's overall brief was ambitious and extensive (DfES, 2005b). While it included some market-based elements, others seemed to respond to the potentially negative effects of such policies. It was consistent with the New Labour emphasis on standards, and recognized the importance of concerted collective efforts to raise achievement among those schools and children that had been languishing under existing policies. The first Commissioner for London Schools, Tim Brighouse, describes London as trying to be the first place to show that schools could contribute to 'cracking the cycle of disadvantage' (Brighouse, 2007: 79).

London Challenge was initially a five-year partnership between central government, schools and boroughs to raise standards in London's secondary school system. Provision included transforming some failing schools into academies, pan-London resources and programmes available to all schools, individualized support for the most disadvantaged pupils and intensive work with five of the 33 London boroughs and more particularly with 'Keys to Success' schools within them. These schools were those in London facing the biggest challenges and in greatest need of additional support. Each school received bespoke solutions through diagnostic work and ongoing support (Brighouse, 2007). Provision was extended in 2006 to include work with primary schools and in relation to pupils' progression to further and higher education. There has been additional continuing professional development for teachers through the Chartered London Teacher scheme and for head teachers or principals through the London Leadership Strategy.

The Conservative Secretary of State for Education from 2010 to 2014, Michael Gove, claimed that the three most important elements in London's success were sponsored academies, the use of outstanding schools to mentor others and a focus on improving the quality of teaching, especially through Teach First (Gove, 2012). While this emphasis is perhaps not surprising given the centrality of these particular policies to his own party's preferred reforms, which are discussed at the end of this paper, there is certainly some support for the claim that each of these particular policies had a positive impact on schools in their own right (Machin and Vernoit, 2011; Earley and Weindling, 2006; Muijs *et al.*, 2010). However, we are not aware of any research that shows that they were necessarily the most important elements in the success of London Challenge or in narrowing the attainment gap in London. In reality, New Labour's London Challenge programme, whose success Gove was praising, was a multi-faceted and system-wide policy, and it included some elements that seem to be out of step with the present government's approach. It involved a range of interventions at the level of 'the London teacher, the London leader, the London school and the London student' (Brighouse, 2007: 80ff).

This means that, unfortunately, as with national policies, it is actually quite difficult to identify which, if any, of the particular parts of the intervention did make a difference. Nevertheless, many commentators have suggested that the overall approach of London Challenge does seem to have had an impact. They point to national performance data that show that from 2003 to 2006 the national rate of improvement in the number of pupils achieving five or more GCSE passes with grades A*–C at age 16 was 6.7 per cent, whereas in London it was 8.4 per cent and in the 'Keys to Success' schools in London it was 12.9 per cent (DfES, 2007a).

Towards the end of its existence, London Challenge was extended to other English cities as City Challenge (DfES, 2007b). Hutchings *et al.* (2012) suggest that these programmes had impacts on reducing the number of underperforming schools and increasing the performance of those pupils eligible for FSM faster than the national average. However, only in London (and in Greater Manchester in the primary phase) was there a closing of the attainment gap over the period 2008–11.

Even in London, it was initially suggested that the improvement in the overall performance of London schools noted above derived largely from an increase in attainment among the more advantaged pupils in the schools that were receiving the most intensive interventions. However, subsequently it was found that not only were the 'Keys to Success' schools improving at a faster rate than the norm, the attainment gap for disadvantaged children in London was itself narrowing faster than elsewhere and in these particular schools narrowing fastest of all. Using FSM entitlement as a proxy for economic disadvantage, data provided to us by the DfES showed that attainment at age 16 for this group of pupils within 'Keys to Success' schools rose by a larger amount than for the non-FSM pupils (13.1 percentage points, compared to 12.3 points for the latter between 2003 and 2006). Michael Gove too drew attention to this particular success for poorer children in London when he noted that while in England more generally '35 per cent of children on free school meals achieve five good GCSEs with English and Maths ... in inner-London 52 per cent meet [this benchmark]' (Gove, 2012). He also noted that this is not far off the national average for pupils regardless of their background.

An inspection report from Ofsted on the impact of London Challenge described continuing positive impacts beyond the initial period. It noted that the primary schools that joined London Challenge 'are improving faster than those in the rest of England', partly attributing this to schools continuing to participate in development programmes for teachers after the support given as part of London Challenge had ended (Ofsted, 2010a). The report was positive about the possibilities for maintaining the gains from London Challenge due to changes it has engendered in practices (such as increased use of performance data to track progress) and ethos (such as motivating staff to share good practice with other schools). It could be that such collaboration may have countered the more negative effects of school choice mechanisms, so it will be important to monitor what happens in London now that the initiative as a whole has finally come to an end but market-oriented policies remain in place. On this issue, Hutchings *et al.* (2012) found some encouraging evidence that schools that were part of the initial London Challenge scheme, but no longer funded as Keys to Success schools after 2008, continued to improve at a faster rate than the national average despite the extra support ending.

However, it is possible that there were also other factors at work in London that contributed to progress in the capital under New Labour (Wyness, 2011; Allen, 2012). Indeed, various reports in 2014 on the improvement in the educational performance of London, and the role of London Challenge in that improvement, came to significantly different conclusions. These varied from lauding the impact of London Challenge (Baars *et al.*, 2014) to explaining the success by earlier educational interventions (Greaves *et al.*, 2014), and attributing it to the changing ethnic mix of the capital (Burgess, 2014). The controversy continues to this day (McAleavy and Elwick, 2015; Blanden *et al.*, 2015), but this issue requires resolution before we can assume that policies associated with London Challenge are replicable (even with contextual adjustments) in other parts of the country, as has been suggested by Ofsted (2013c) and Policy Forum (Claeys *et al.*, 2014).

After all, it can plausibly be argued – rather as Diane Ravitch (2010) argues in the case of New York School District 2 – that even the limited progress made under New Labour, particularly in London, had more to do with their tenure of office coinciding with a period of sustained economic boom and demographic changes than with any of these education policies, so that perhaps the economy is the driver and Bernstein (1970) was right after all that education cannot compensate for society. If this is the case it will be much more of a challenge to bring about similar improvements in the post-industrial cities of the North of England or the run-down seaside towns that have more recently become the focus of education policy.

'Closing the gap'? The Conservative–Liberal Democrat Coalition, 2010–15

The Coalition Government that was elected to replace New Labour in May 2010 made an even more ambitious commitment to 'closing' the achievement gap as part of a wider drive to increase social mobility, which it claimed had stalled under New Labour (HM Government, 2010a). The general thrust of their policies was to continue and accelerate the emphasis on seeking improvement through school autonomy, competition and choice that was pioneered by Margaret Thatcher's Conservative government but continued by New Labour under Tony Blair (Whitty 1989, 2008).

While the academies policy of the Blair government discussed above sought to use academy status mainly to prioritize the replacement or improvement of failing schools in disadvantaged areas, the Conservative-led Coalition extended this status potentially to virtually all schools. Schools highly rated by Ofsted, a disproportionate number of which are in more affluent areas, can be granted academy status automatically if they so desire. A recent finding from research on earlier academies, that significant improvements occurred only for schools experiencing a large increase in their autonomy relative to their predecessor status, may mean that the more privileged schools converting in recent years will not see the same benefits (Eyles and Machin, 2015). However, the policy of conversion proceeds apace as the majority Conservative Government elected in 2015 has announced that more schools are to be permitted or required to adopt academy status. Meanwhile, parents, teachers and others have been encouraged by the Coalition Government and its Conservative successor to open publicly funded 'free schools', which, like academies, will be outside local authority jurisdiction.

It remains an open question whether such policies will help to close the gap or, as some critics have suggested, effectively open it up again, and recent attempts to assess the evidence have come to no firm conclusions about the impact of these policies (House of Commons, 2015; McNally, 2015). So far around sixty per cent of English secondary schools and nearly 10 per cent of primary schools have academy or free school status, and increasingly many of them are being linked in academy 'chains', whose performance, like that of stand-alone academies, is variable particularly in respect of closing the gap (Hutchings *et al.*, 2014, 2015). Just as Curtis *et al.* (2008) argued that academies were not a panacea, Hutchings *et al.* (2015) say the same about academy chains.

Recognizing that there is a complex relationship between attainment, autonomy, collaboration and accountability, the House of Commons Education Select Committee argued towards the end of the Coalition Government that 'current evidence does not allow us to draw conclusions on whether academies in themselves are a positive force for change' and 'agree[d] with Ofsted that it is too early to draw conclusions on the quality of education provided by free schools or their broader system impact' (House of Commons, 2015). Nevertheless, a controversial study by the right-leaning think tank Policy Exchange has since suggested that, contrary to some of the criticisms levelled at free schools, their presence has improved rather than diminished the results of poorly performing neighbouring schools (Porter and Simons, 2015). The sample sizes, let alone this argument's ideological provenance, make this a less than convincing demonstration of the benefits of competition, but it is certainly a finding that would merit more rigorous investigation. R. Morris (2015) reports mixed results from an investigation of whether free schools are taking their fair share of disadvantaged children.

As mentioned earlier, a major thrust of policy under the Coalition Government was to identify and address achievement gaps outside the large conurbations. Some of these underperforming areas have been in apparently affluent areas in counties such as Surrey in the south of England, but media attention has often become focused on small northern cities, small towns in the east of England and coastal towns around the country (Ofsted, 2013c). It has certainly been important to highlight previously neglected underperformance in such areas and remind ourselves that the achievement gap is (and has always been in practice) much more than a 'urban' problem in the conventional sense. Not only are there more disadvantaged children outside 'failing' schools in the big cities, but they are often 'unseen' for a variety of reasons that require careful study. However, the main policy solutions have been familiar, namely academization and a series of local and regional challenges (Ovenden-Hope and Passy, 2013; Claeys *et al.*, 2014). It will be important for any such future initiatives to be aligned to particular local demographic and economic conditions rather than mimicking the apparent success of London Challenge (and, to a lesser extent, the other City Challenges) of the New Labour era.

There exists also considerable controversy about whether the government's curriculum policies will help to close the gap. There was, for example, a commendable emphasis on early literacy but an undue commitment to 'synthetic phonics' as the only way to teach reading, despite research evidence that, while it can indeed be an effective strategy with disadvantaged children, it is not a panacea and that a more mixed approach is desirable (Wyse and Parker, 2012).

Another policy introduced by Michael Gove, when Secretary of State for Education in the Coalition Government, was the English Baccalaureate (EBacc), an award (but not a qualification) for pupils but also effectively a new performance measure for secondary schools based on the percentage of pupils achieving high grades in specified subjects, that is, English, maths, science, history or geography, and a foreign language.[2] This seems, initially at least, to have affected socially disadvantaged pupils adversely, as they are more likely to have been exposed to alternative curricula than more advantaged pupils on a university entrance track, and this policy seems at least in the short term to have contributed to opening up the achievement gap again (DfE, 2014a).[3]

A linked policy has been to reduce the number of 'equivalent' qualifications that are permitted to be used in school performance tables as alternatives to the GCSE qualifications at age 16. This will have an impact on the number of vocational qualifications taught in schools and places a further emphasis on a return to conventional academic qualifications. Ironically, in view of the Coalition Government's enthusiastic embrace of the academies programme, some of the New Labour academies that moved sharply up the performance tables in recent years did so partly by introducing these alternative qualifications (de Waal, 2009).

The Coalition Government's response to concerns about its traditionalist curriculum policy was that social justice required equal access to high-status knowledge, and that there was little point in pupils succeeding on courses that are deemed to have little value by universities, employers and the wider society. However, while there may well be a good argument for ensuring that all pupils should have the opportunity to gain access to 'powerful knowledge' (Young, 2010), if indeed that is what the traditional curriculum provides, governments will need to give more attention than they have done hitherto to reforming the pedagogy through which those subjects are taught. Exley and Ball (2011) argue that some recent policies have involved a return to the nineteenth century, and we do need to remember that very few disadvantaged children and families benefited from the type of schooling that predominated in those days.[5]

Some of the neo-conservative policies advocated by the Conservatives were moderated under the 2010–15 Coalition Government by the social justice agenda of the Liberal Democrat Party whose votes gave the Coalition its majority in parliament. Among policies that were strongly influenced by Liberal Democrat thinking, albeit with some Conservative support, was a commitment to address the attainment gap through a 'pupil premium' to be paid, on top of the normal grant, for every school-age state school student in receipt of free school meals. This was consistent with the earlier trend of linking resources to individuals in need regardless of the neighbourhood in which they are receiving their schooling. Unfortunately, welcome as this payment has been, its level is significantly below that envisaged by the Liberal Democrats prior to the 2010 election, and it replaced some other targeted benefits that were paid under New Labour. Most seriously, the fact that it was introduced at a time of major expenditure cuts in other areas means that some schools barely noticed its impact. Nevertheless, it was significantly increased and extended during the course of the last parliament and, although the money was not ring-fenced or mandated for particular purposes, monitoring of its use by Ofsted seems to have helped ensure that it was used in many schools to benefit the education of disadvantaged pupils.

Although early surveys were not particularly encouraging in this respect, and suggested that too little of the money allocated through the pupil premium for disadvantaged children had been spent on activities that were known to boost attainment (The Sutton Trust, 2012; Ofsted, 2012), more recent surveys have been somewhat more positive about its role in narrowing the gap (Ofsted, 2014a). The introduction by Ofsted of a specific performance indicator for narrowing the gap, together with the government's use of a 'progression' measure alongside the traditional five A*–C GCSEs achievement measure in holding schools to account, added to the pressure on schools to use the funding for this purpose.

An initiative that was intended to help them do so was the creation by the Coalition Government of the Education Endowment Foundation (EEF), the grant-making charity whose work was mentioned in Chapter 1. This was dedicated to raising the attainment of disadvantaged pupils. Its Learning and Teaching Toolkit first launched in 2012 (EEF, 2012) provided specific guidance to schools on how best to use the pupil premium to improve the attainment of their pupils, drawing on relevant research from the United Kingdom and elsewhere. It identified effective feedback, meta-cognition and peer tutoring as three strategies that had been shown to have high or very high impact at low cost, on the basis of strong evidence. In the case of peer tutoring it suggested that children from disadvantaged backgrounds derived particularly large benefits from this strategy. The EEF has subsequently funded a number of new research projects to enhance the evidence base.

But, although some of this work may have made a difference, its achievements may turn out to be of marginal significance in the longer run. There are already signs that the slight narrowing of the attainment gap identified earlier under New Labour has stalled or even been reversed, at least at secondary school level (DfE, 2014a; Ofsted, 2014b). While this may have been a reflection of the wider effects of economic austerity as much as specific education policies brought in by the Coalition Government (Clifton and Cook, 2012), the downgrading of vocational and alternative courses in accountability measures mentioned above does seem to have had a significant impact (Adams, 2015).

A further issue is that the gap on what are being termed 'elite measures' remains stubbornly wide, as illustrated in Figure 4.4 below.

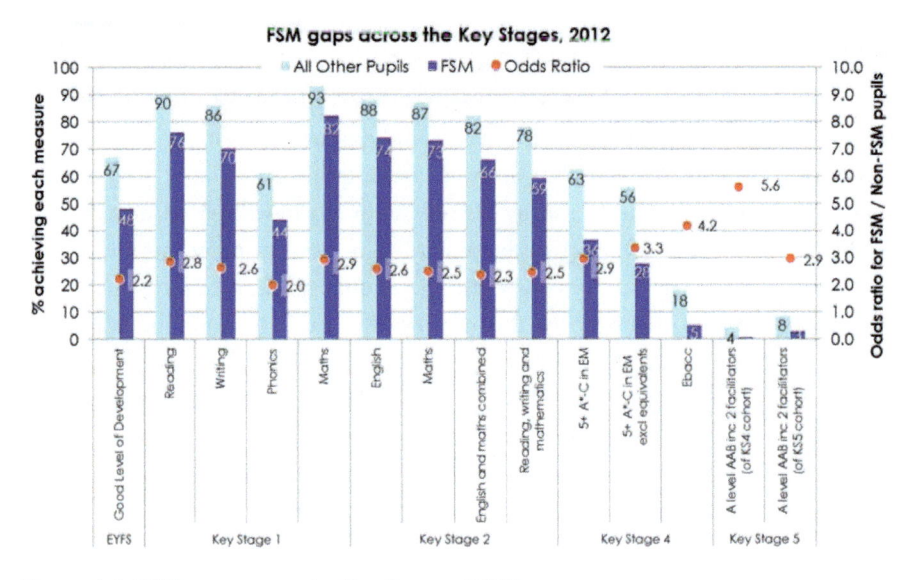

Figure 4.4: FSM gaps across the Key Stages (2012)

Source: DfE (2013), personal communication.

This shows that, even where the attainment gap in schools has narrowed overall, it is largest for the elite measures, Levels 5 and 6 at KS2, five A*–C at KS4 and AAB at A-level (even after drop-out). Given the crucial importance of these and other elite measures for social sorting, via entry to the upper reaches of higher education and the professions, the challenge remains considerable. It is almost as if, as one gap begins to narrow, the goalposts are moved, as Gillborn (2014) puts it in relation to what he calls the 'Black/White' gap. This is hardly surprising to those who have studied sociology, especially the work by Bowles and Gintis (1976) and Bourdieu and Passeron (1977) on the role of education in social and cultural reproduction.[6]

If further progress is to be made in contesting and interrupting the reproductive outcomes of education, what is needed, at the very least, is an acceptance of the conclusion of Kerr and West (2010: 41) that 'efforts to improve schools must be accompanied by efforts to support disadvantaged families'. This was also the thrust of reports produced for the Coalition Government by Labour MPs Frank Field (2010) and Graham Allen (2011), but only partially acted upon. Furthermore, as was argued under a previous government, 'society needs to be clearer about what schools can and cannot be expected to do' (Mortimore and Whitty, 1997: 12). This does not mean that schools cannot make a difference, or that they do not have a particularly important role in helping to narrow the attainment gap and thereby enhancing the life chances of disadvantaged children. It does mean that they cannot do it alone. The analysis of the impact of English education policy since 1997 offered here also provides support for the warning made by Ravitch (2010: 3) in relation to parallel policies in the USA 'that, in education, there are no shortcuts, no utopias, and no silver bullets'. Unfortunately, there is little evidence that English politicians of any political persuasion have yet learnt those lessons.

Notes

[1] Gillborn was quoted (or misquoted) in Ward (2015: 10) as saying, 'If you want to focus on [the attainment gap between children on free school meals and their peers] that's fine. But then you are taking a decision that you don't care about race inequality'. Such a criticism might be applied to this chapter, but we would argue that it would not be a fair one. Gillborn rightly went on to claim that 'you have to be cognisant of the way in which inequalities interact. It's complicated.' Indeed it is. Hence the insistence in this book that education policy needs to be informed by the sociology of education. This must include current theories of intersectionality (Bhopal and Preston, 2011; Gillborn, 2015).

[2] The majority Conservative Government elected in May 2015 has announced that 90 per cent of pupils who start secondary school in England in September 2015 will have to take all the EBacc subjects when they sit their GCSEs in 2020. Even before that, the Coalition reforms seem to have had an effect, as there was a rise in the number of pupils in England taking traditional GCSEs and A-levels in the 2015 examinations (Sellgren, 2015).

[3] Interestingly, Gillborn has shown that what he calls 'moving the goalposts' has had similar effects on the Black/White achievement gap. He suggests that 'a clear pattern can be seen ... Black Caribbean pupils begin to narrow the gap but the introduction of a new benchmark restores inequality to historic levels ... Introduction of the EBacc, in 2011, restored White odds of success to 2.20 (more than double the Black rate), a rate not seen since 2003.' As a result 'the odds of Black success relative to White peers in 2013 ... is the same as it was back in 2007' (Gillborn, 2014).

[4] The House of Commons Science and Technology Committee has suggested that the roll-out of Reading Recovery pre-dated rigorous evidence of its effectiveness. This is not surprising in view of the different influences on policymaking identified in earlier chapters of this book. The Committee 'found that the Government's use of Reading Recovery is based on evidence, but a lower quality of evidence than we, as a Science and Technology Committee, are comfortable with. The Government's decision to roll out Reading Recovery nationally to the exclusion of other kinds of literacy interventions was, however, not evidence-based, and we have suggested that the Government should commission some high quality research, such as randomised controlled trials, in this area' (House of Commons Science and Technology Committee, 2009).

[5] For a retrospective assessment of Coalition policies, see the special issue 'Education policy under the 2010–15 UK Coalition Government: Critical perspectives', Issue 13 (2) of *London Review of Education*, published 18 September 2015.

[6] Evidence of a 'class ceiling' (Laurison and Friedman, 2015) that affects the progress even of university graduates from lower socio-economic backgrounds is discussed in Chapter 5.

Chapter 5
'Knowing the ropes'?
Access to higher education in England
with Annette Hayton and Sarah Tang

Introduction

Access to higher education in England was still very much a minority pursuit until the 1960s. The shift from an elite to a mass system of higher education only began just over 50 years ago (Trow, 1974; Scott, 1995), when the Robbins Report articulated what came to be known as the Robbins principle that:

> Courses of higher education should be available for all those who are qualified by ability and attainment to pursue them and who wish to do so.
> (Robbins, 1963: 8)

The economic conditions and meritocratic beliefs of the post-war years brought about an overall rise in participation. However, the small numbers of working-class students who progressed on to higher education demonstrated that expansion was not enough to ensure equal access.

From 1970, there was a considerable and persistent gap in the rates of participation in higher education in England between those from higher and lower socio-economic groups – a gap of 25 to 30 percentage points. This is illustrated in Figure 5.1 below.

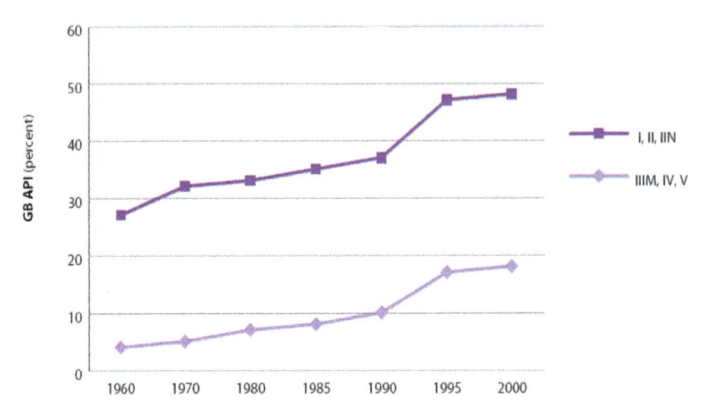

Figure 5.1: Higher education entrants by social class group (1960–2000)

Note: This social class classification is broken down as follows: I: professional, etc. occupations; II: managerial and technical occupations; IIIN: skilled occupations – non-manual; IIIM: skilled occupations: manual; IV: partly skilled occupations; V: unskilled occupations.

Source: DfES (2003) (see also Kelly and Cook, 2007).

New Labour policies

The New Labour Government that was elected in 1997 championed the role of education in developing a high skills workforce and promoting social justice (Wilkins and Burke, 2013). It had two prongs to its policy. The first, *widening participation*, was primarily concerned with narrowing the participation gap in the system as a whole. The second prong, *fair access*, indicated a need to widen participation at elite universities whose admissions policies had often been accused of being biased in favour of pupils from elite private schools (Bekhradnia, 2003).

In 2001, Prime Minister Tony Blair embraced a new ambition to increase the participation of 18–30 year olds in higher education to 50 per cent by 2010. From 2002 all English universities were required to develop and publish a Widening Participation Strategy in return for widening participation funding. In 2004 most existing outreach and other widening participation initiatives were expanded and incorporated into Aimhigher, a major national initiative based on local partnerships that sought to increase participation in higher education through outreach work, in order to raise aspirations among previously under-represented groups.

The issue of access soon became tied up with debates about the funding of higher education more generally, as upfront tuition fees of £1,000 had been introduced in 1998 and from 2006 universities could choose to charge a maximum of £3,000 per year. Recognizing that one of the risks of this policy, particularly for a Labour Government publicly committed to social justice, was that students from poorer backgrounds would be put off higher education, maintenance grants, which had been abolished in 1998, were reintroduced for poorer students in 2004. In the same year, an Office for Fair Access (OFFA) was established and all universities planning to charge the new 'top-up' fees were required to produce an Access Agreement setting out their plans for widening participation (DfES, 2003; OFFA, 2004)

Although there was resistance to imposing quotas on universities, each university was given an individual widening participation benchmark that was calculated by taking into account the range of subjects offered at the institution and the entry qualification of the students recruited.

Performance against targets

There have been various attempts to evaluate New Labour's performance by considering the extent to which quantitative inequality and qualitative inequality were reduced during its period of office (Boliver, 2008). In broad terms, the first is a measure of widening participation, the second of fair access.

Quantitative inequality

In 2007, the government revised the methodology it used to measure the participation gap (Kelly and Cook, 2007). This new measure showed a more positive picture, with the participation gap declining since the mid-1990s and standing at 20.2 per cent in 2007/8, as can be seen in Figure 5.2.

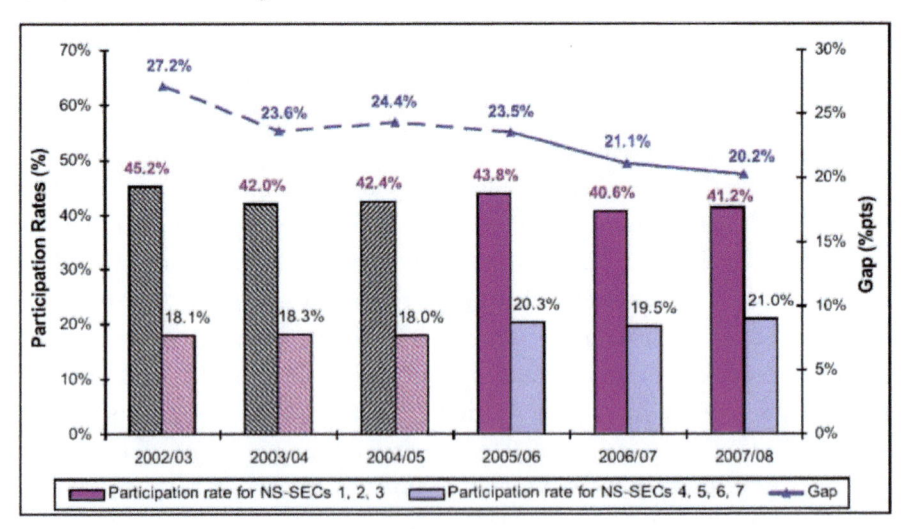

Figure 5.2: Participation rates (FYPSEC) of those from high and low socio-economic backgrounds and their gap (2002–8)

Note: This figure shows the Full-time Young Participation by Socio-Economic Class (FYPSEC) measure. FYPSEC covers English-domiciled 18- to 20-year-old first-time entrants to full-time higher education at UK HEIs and English further education (FE) colleges who remain on their courses for at least six months.

Source: BIS (2009c).

However, other research carried out at that time showed major disparities and differences in participation between diverse social groups when you dug beneath the surface (David, 2010). It is thus important to consider participation in a more nuanced way than simply comparing participation rates from higher and lower socio-economic groups or neighbourhoods.

Qualitative inequality

Even if participation rates from lower socio-economic status (SES) groups do increase overall, the so-called theory of Effectively Maintained Inequality (EMI) suggests that those groups who had previously had more exclusive access to higher education will maintain their advantage by seeking out supposedly 'better' education (Lucas, 2001). It does not actually have to be better than elsewhere, but people have to believe it is. In England, more affluent families maintain their positional advantage by attending highly prestigious institutions at which students from a low SES background are a rarity (Curtis *et al.*, 2008). As has been said of a similar phenomenon in the USA,

'Knowing the ropes'?

'student access to the system as a whole does not mean access to the whole system' (Bastedo and Gumport, 2003: 355).

Using data from 2001/2 – part way through New Labour's time in office – Boliver (2008) pointed to the uneven distribution of students from different socio-economic groups across different types of university, with 20 per cent of entrants to 'old' universities coming from professional families compared to 10 per cent of those going to 'new' universities.[1] Figure 5.3 shows the uneven distribution of students in a different way, with 44 per cent of students in higher education from professional families attending Russell Group universities but only 23 per cent of those from unskilled backgrounds doing so.

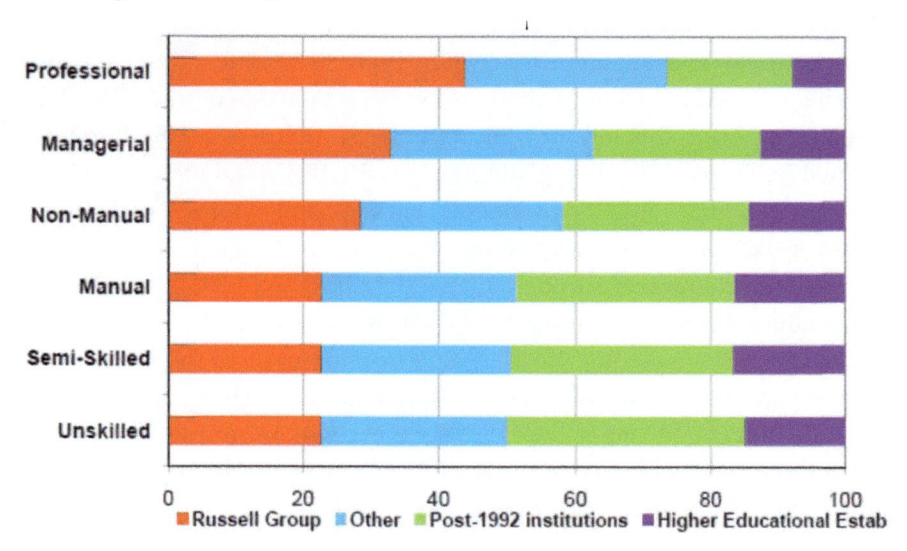

Figure 5.3: Type of university attended by socio-economic background

Note: 'Other' refers to pre-1992 universities that were not members of the Russell Group at the time. 'Higher Educational Estab[lishments]' means here 'non-vocational institutions that have yet to be awarded university status'.

Source: (Hills *et al.*, 2010).

Boliver (2013) subsequently extended her analysis to cover the years 1996 to 2006, and found that throughout the period applicants from lower social class backgrounds and from state schools were less likely to apply to Russell Group universities than their peers from higher social class backgrounds and private schools, and that those from state schools and certain minority ethnic groups (though not from lower social class backgrounds as such) were less likely than their peers to receive offers. She therefore concluded that access to Russell Group universities was still 'far from fair' (Boliver, 2013: 344).

The more fine-grained the distinctions between universities, the more noticeable was the social gradient and access to the most prestigious higher education institutions was still dominated by those from elite private schools. In 2007, 46.6 per cent of young, full-time, first-degree entrants to the University of Oxford came from private schools (HESA, 2009). This figure was all the more striking when you consider that only about 7 per cent of English children are educated in such schools (DCSF, 2008). Analysis undertaken by The Sutton Trust, a UK charity working to improve social mobility through education, which looked at participation in selective universities specifically, suggested that around 30 per cent of students at what it regarded as the most prestigious universities (the 'Sutton 13') came from just 200 schools (out of a total of around 3,700 secondary schools and colleges).[2] It further found that just under half of the students at Oxford and Cambridge came from just 200 schools (The Sutton Trust, 2008).

It would appear, then, that while there was some progress in widening participation under New Labour, there remained considerable qualitative inequalities. Even though the different measures used in the various studies outlined below produce slightly different results, the broad picture is clear. Harris (2010) found that, although widening participation efforts had had a positive impact overall, the picture was different if the group of what the report calls 'highly selective' institutions was considered separately. It showed that, although the overall higher education participation rate of the least advantaged 40 per cent of students had increased since the mid-1990s, the participation rate of the same group at the most selective third of universities had stayed constant. The gap between the most and least advantaged had actually increased in these universities as those from the most advantaged backgrounds (the top 20 per cent) were now more likely to attend these institutions than they were in the mid-1990s.

A somewhat more positive picture can be derived from work by Crawford (2012) and Chowdry et al. (2013), which not only shows a significant narrowing of the socio-economic gap in entry to higher education overall between 2004/5 and 2010/11, but also some narrowing of the gap at 'high status universities' during this period, partly driven by a slight fall in participation among the most advantaged students.[3] On the other hand, the Social Mobility and Child Poverty Commission set up by the Coalition Government found that the proportion of students from state schools who started full-time courses in Russell Group universities fell slightly between 2002/3 and 2011/12, while a separate measure of how many students came from disadvantaged backgrounds also saw a fall (SMCPC, 2013).

A report from OFFA (2014) using area-based data seemed to confirm that limited progress was made in tackling qualitative inequality as compared to quantitative inequality during the New Labour period and indeed beyond. Thus, while participation of the most disadvantaged at low- and medium-entry-tariff institutions showed a significant improvement during that period, there was no equivalent change at high-entry-tariff institutions (Harris, 2010; OFFA, 2014).[4] However, we should note that a time lag may have been in operation, as the most recent 'end-of-cycle' publication from Universities and Colleges Admissions Services (UCAS) shows a marked improvement in this area. It reports that 'young people from the most disadvantaged areas in 2014 were around 40% more likely to enter higher tariff institutions than three years ago' (UCAS, 2014), albeit from a low base. It seems that increased institutional accountability and more stringent regulation of universities from OFFA may have had some effect, despite the unpopularity of such measures in some quarters.

Nevertheless, taken together, the data presented here suggest that, despite widening participation in higher education as a whole, New Labour's attempts to ensure fair access had only modest success to date. Some commentators have criticized the premises underlying New Labour policies – for example, those of Aimhigher – for focusing on the assumed deficits of individuals rather than structural issues (Gewirtz, 2001; Archer and Leathwood, 2003; Burke, 2012). Yet, without the changes in awareness brought about by Aimhigher and similar provisions amongst prospective students, their families and their teachers, change might have been far slower (Doyle and Griffin, 2012). Collaboration between institutions through Aimhigher in particular allowed for more efficient targeting of resources and its focus on widening participation in general instilled confidence in schools and colleges that HEIs' efforts to increase progression to higher education were not merely part of a recruitment drive for a particular institution. While Aimhigher had many limitations, it should be noted that few universities had seriously engaged in outreach work targeting under-represented groups before these New Labour initiatives.

Coalition and Conservative government policies

The Conservative-led Coalition Government that took office in 2010 received a report on the future of funding of higher education from the Browne review, which had been established by its New Labour predecessor. Although the recommendations of the Browne Report were not adopted in full, they were pivotal in paving the way for the most radical change in the funding of UK higher education for the last 40 years, accelerating the move away from direct public funding of universities towards financing through fee income. The introduction of an increased maximum fee of £9,000, not paid up-front by the student but recovered later through an income-contingent loan, was highly contested in parliament and the subject of fierce resistance from students. A number of concessions designed to enhance social mobility were made, and these were essential to maintain the coalition with the Liberal Democrat Party, which had previously opposed the charging of tuition fees. A National Scholarship Programme was introduced, providing fee waivers for academically able students from poorer backgrounds (HEFCE, 2011b). The powers of OFFA were increased and Les Ebdon, the former Vice-Chancellor of a post-1992 university, was appointed as its new Director. This created anxiety amongst selective universities, and accusations from Conservative members of a parliamentary select committee that his policies were a recipe for social engineering and the dumbing down of higher education (Paton, 2012). Universities charging over £6,000 in fees were required to produce an Access Agreement showing how they would enhance their strategies to assist students from under-represented groups by providing financial support, ensuring fair admissions, delivering outreach activities and improving student retention.

These measures, combined with the closure of Aimhigher, resulted in a significant change in the way that university outreach activities were funded and delivered. The increased focus on the performance of individual universities in reaching their widening participation recruitment benchmarks stimulated more energetic outreach and admissions measures in selective universities than was previously seen. However, the loss of the collaborative planning framework afforded by Aimhigher resulted in many schools and colleges losing the links with higher education that they had previously enjoyed. Equally controversially, the Coalition abolished the Education Maintenance Allowance (EMA) for 16–19 year olds in education, along with the Connexions careers provision. A new online careers service for adults was introduced but there was no specified provision for 16–18 year olds. Responsibility for information, advice and guidance (IAG) for this age group has been devolved to schools and colleges, raising serious concerns about inequalities in provision particularly for students without strong family and community traditions of entering higher education (House of Commons Education Select Committee, 2013). The new arrangements have also been criticized by Ofsted (2013) for creating a patchy and inconsistent pattern of provision, which could leave children in some schools without appropriate advice.

Because the Coalition parties were unable to agree the terms of a new Higher Education Bill, much of the government's policymaking on higher education was necessarily ad hoc. Nevertheless, its flagship White Paper was clearly titled – *Students at the Heart of the System* – and the Coalition also remained publicly committed to its post-election pledge to increase social mobility and attract 'a higher proportion of students from disadvantaged backgrounds' (HM Government, 2010a: 31–2). Meanwhile, the Coalition's reforms to the schools system were far-reaching, including in their implications for progression to university.

The government's decision to reform national school examinations at both GCSE and A-level (usually taken at ages 16 and 18, respectively), and to restrict the number of alternative qualifications that count in school and college performance tables, as mentioned in Chapter 4, may make it harder for students from non-traditional backgrounds to achieve the grades necessary to gain entry to university. Nevertheless, this removal of recognition for some vocational qualifications, following the Wolf Report (2011), could arguably clarify which qualifications they need in order to gain admission, as there is a clear advantage in taking 'traditional' subjects (Iannelli, 2013).[5] The Coalition Government anyway took the view that university is not necessarily the right aspiration for all school leavers. Consequently, it – and the majority Conservative Government that succeeded it – espoused apprenticeships, both in their own right and as an alternative route to university.[6]

The Department for Education has also introduced destinations data, including entry to Russell Group universities, as a new performance indicator for secondary schools. This may suggest that it does not value other universities. Such an outlook may also have been reflected in the decision by the Department for Business, Innovation & Skills (BIS) to allow universities to recruit as many high-achieving students (initially those with AAB grades in Advanced or 'A-level' examinations but subsequently extended to ABB grades) as they could, insofar as it is the more selective universities that attract the vast majority of such applicants.

At this stage, it is unclear what effect these various policies will have in practice on widening participation and fair access. What Callender and Scott (2013) rightly portray as a strongly contested higher fees regime has not actually resulted in a reduction in applications from school leavers on the scale predicted (ICOF, 2014; UCAS, 2014). Nor does the change seem to have disproportionately affected entry to higher education by disadvantaged students in the younger age group. On the other hand, concerns about persistent qualitative inequalities have remained (The Sutton Trust, 2014) and some of the Coalition's later policies (and those of the Conservative Government that succeeded it in 2015) have reinforced equity concerns.

First, it was announced that the National Scholarship Programme (NSP), introduced earlier in response to demands from Liberal Democrat Party members of the Coalition, would be abandoned for undergraduate students from 2015, and HEFCE funding to universities would be reduced disproportionately for post-1992 universities, which serve large numbers of students from under-represented groups. There also seems to have been a marked shift in some institutions away from generic widening participation to a 'focus on the brightest poor students' (McCaig, 2016: 215), a finding confirmed by the Institute for Fiscal Studies (Dearden and Jin, 2014).

Then, in December 2013, Chancellor of the Exchequer George Osborne unexpectedly announced that student numbers would be increased by 30,000 for 2014/15 and that student number controls would be ended from 2015/16 onwards. Although potentially welcome news for widening access to the system as a whole, the detailed effects of this change remain unpredictable (Hillman, 2014). There is a possibility that expansion could be concentrated mainly in the post-1992 universities, while more traditional institutions with significant research income choose to maintain their present size and status, making competition for entry to them even tighter, to the potential detriment of applicants from disadvantaged families and schools. On the other hand, if, as looks likely, at least some traditional high-tariff universities do expand significantly, they could cream off high-achieving disadvantaged students from post-1992 universities. Either scenario could potentially result in the effective recreation of the binary system that existed prior to 1992. There are also concerns about the quality of the student experience in the context of growing student numbers and a decreasing unit of resource, which in turn may lead to renewed calls to raise the level of the cap on fees.[7]

Despite these dangers, it was encouraging for widening participation that, in a period of reduced public funding overall, £22m was earmarked by the Coalition Government for universities to develop collaborative outreach activities to ensure contact with universities for all schools and colleges. This new National Network for Collaborative Outreach (HEFCE, 2014a) has come largely in response to a growing recognition of some negative outcomes arising from the closure of Aimhigher, most notably the existence of groups of schools lacking direct contact with a university. As universities have increasingly focused their outreach activities on schools that will enable them to meet their own performance indicators for widening participation, some schools have been neglected. The intention now is that every secondary school in England will have a single point of contact. There remains, however, a case for better national coordination of access initiatives. HEFCE (2015) reports that, while there is good work going on in individual institutions, it is 'fragmented', and there is a lack of detailed evidence on which interventions achieve the best results for different groups.

For the time being, the majority Conservative Government elected in May 2015 is continuing the approach of the Coalition, but one of its few new policy announcements at the time of writing has been the abolition of remaining maintenance grants, making virtually the whole of the student finance system loan-based from 2016 onwards. Fears have been expressed that this will discourage disadvantaged students through the prospect of an additional £11,000 debt on graduation, and it has been suggested that this may have caused a surge in late applications in 2015 from candidates seeking to avoid the impact of the new policy (Garner, 2015).

Whatever the emerging shape and character of the higher education system in the coming years, widening participation and fair access are likely to remain major issues for the foreseeable future. The current National Strategy for Access and Student Success announced in April 2014 (BIS, 2014) takes a student lifecycle approach and identifies three broad stages: access (encompassing outreach activities and admissions), retention and student success, and progression into further study and employment. Its clear focus on evaluation is an important development for widening participation but it will be some years before we can make any firm judgements about the impact of current and future activities.

Barriers to participation and fair access

It remains important to review what we currently know about the continuing barriers to participation and access with a view to identifying what else might be done to ensure more equitable access to higher education. In so doing, we recognize that there are limitations in removing barriers if we do not 'change the nature of whatever it is that people are meant to be participating in' (Gorard and See, 2013: 102), but we take the view that enhancing equality of opportunity to access the current system is a necessary, although not a sufficient, ambition for our society.

Since well before the publication of the Robbins Report in 1963, finance has usually been seen as the main barrier preventing students from under-represented groups accessing higher education. This is one of the reasons why funding issues have been at the heart of debates over higher education policy. In the next part of this paper we explore the various economic, social and cultural factors that lead to differential participation in higher education. While the term 'barrier' has been justifiably criticized by Burke (2012) when used to focus attention on the so-called inadequacies of prospective students, that is not what we intend here. Indeed, we begin by exploring the material impact of insufficient financial resources, something that Burke herself agrees is a real 'barrier'. We then go on to explore aspirations and awareness, and attainment, and discuss how these factors relate to the social and cultural capitals accessible to those from under-represented groups, and thereby begin to explain the enduring class differences in university admissions.

It is important to contrast our use of the concepts of social and cultural capital with those that underpinned New Labour's social policies, based as they often were on addressing the perceived 'deficits' of individuals and communities (Gamarnikow and Green, 1999; Gewirtz, 2001; Leathwood and Hayton, 2002; Burke 2012). Instead, we follow Bourdieu (1986) who recognizes that social or cultural capitals are expressions of differences in status and power within an unequal social system. In his analysis, economic, social and cultural capitals are all considered in terms of enabling and restricting engagement with education. He also expanded his concept of capitals in relation to education, distinguishing between intellectual or scientific capital (subject expertise), academic capital (understanding of rules and customs within the academy) and social capital (social connections). As we shall see, in those terms, success in educational institutions thus depends not just on 'what you know', but also on 'knowing the ropes' and sometimes, even today, on 'who you know'.

Student finance

There have been concerns at each successive change in fees policy that students from 'non-standard' backgrounds would be particularly adversely affected. Such concerns have received some support from an academic literature that suggests there may be subtle financial inhibitions, particularly affecting those for whom applying for university was already a marginal decision. Some commentators even suggest that there are fundamentally different perceptions about finance among people from different social backgrounds. For example, Burke (2012: 139) claims that 'the willingness to accept debt as an inevitable part of the pursuit of "success" is tied to particular (white, middle-class) values and dispositions'. Certainly, it is often claimed that those from lower socio-economic backgrounds are likely to be more debt-averse (Van Dyke *et al.*, 2005). Callender and Jackson (2008) reported that low-income students are more likely than their wealthier peers to perceive the costs of higher education as a debt rather than an investment. However, Davies *et al.* (2009) did not find evidence of greater debt aversion among disadvantaged students after taking account of school grades and a preference to live at home. Rather, they concluded that any debt aversion arose from the more marginal benefit students with lower grades might expect from higher education (see also Mangan *et al.*, 2010).

While debt aversion may not usually be pivotal in the decision on whether to enter higher education, it may have an impact at the margins, especially for disadvantaged students. A study by the Institute of Employment Studies (BIS, 2010), which looked at the importance of finance in higher education participation decisions, reinforced this picture. It found that while finance did not seem to be a central factor in student intentions, there were differences between those from different backgrounds, with non-traditional students appearing more debt-averse, particularly concerning loans. Callender and Jackson (2008) found that, although finance did not necessarily affect decisions regarding whether to study or even what to study, it did seem to play a role in considerations of where to study.

That young people from lower socio-economic backgrounds are more likely to choose to live at home with their parents both restricts their choice of university and means that they can miss out on other aspects of the traditional residential experience of higher education (Davies *et al.*, 2008; Mangan *et al.*, 2010). It is not clear that the financial assistance available to students is sufficient in contexts where the young person cannot draw on additional support from parents to cover the full costs of attending higher education away from home. It is also the case that students from lower socio-economic backgrounds are more likely than other students to take up part-time paid employment during their time at university (Van Dyke *et al.*, 2005), which could interfere with their academic studies, leading to lower grades through fewer study hours and a greater propensity to drop out.

After HEIs were allowed to charge variable fees, the government expected institutions to spend some of the additional income that would be generated on supporting poorer students through bursaries. In 2006/7, HEIs in England spent approximately a fifth of the additional income they earned through fees on such support. Research by Callender (2010) examining the bursary and institutional support available to students from poorer backgrounds showed that there were considerable differences in terms of bursaries available across HEIs. Each university had a bursary scheme with different criteria and levels of support, creating a very complex system and one that too often introduced new inequities into the system rather than reducing them. The IES study cited earlier found that the level of knowledge and information regarding what financial support was available was low (BIS, 2010; see also Callender, 2009). This supported other research (Davies *et al.*,

2008) that suggested that many bursaries and grants were not being taken up at that time. Dearden and Jin (2014) also comment on the continuing complexity of the system of financial support.

A great deal of the work in this area took place before the new £9,000 fee regime was introduced in 2012, so the impact of that change is only beginning to emerge. As we have seen, the decision of the Coalition Government following the Browne Report to allow maximum fees to rise from around £3,000 to £9,000, funded by income-contingent loans, rang loud alarm bells for those concerned with equitable access to higher education (Garner, 2009). However, although there has been a reduction in overall application rates under the new fees regime (UCAS, 2012, 2014), application rates for young people from more advantaged backgrounds fell by more between 2011 and 2012 than they did among those from less advantaged backgrounds. There was also no discernible tendency for less advantaged students to be more likely to avoid courses charging the highest fees. Although this analysis suggested that the new regime had not disproportionately affected disadvantaged 18-year-olds, there were significant drops (of up to 40 per cent) in applications from mature students and part-time students (UUK, 2013; ICOF, 2014).

Aspiration and awareness

The tendency to position under-represented groups as lacking in aspiration, while central to the prevailing policy discourse on widening participation, has been seriously criticized in much of the sociological literature (Archer *et al.*, 2002; Burke, 2012; Gewirtz, 2001). Even writers more sympathetic to this narrative have queried the strength of the evidence base for the link between socio-economic background, aspiration and attainment (Gorard *et al.*, 2012; Baker *et al.*, 2014). In the context of Aimhigher, work undertaken by Atherton and colleagues at the University of Westminster explored the aspirations of those in Year Seven (the first year of secondary school), and found no lack of aspiration among students from lower SES backgrounds in terms of jobs or higher education (Atherton *et al.*, 2009). Parental aspirations for their children to attend university also appear to be high across all social classes (Centre for Longitudinal Studies, 2010). This work stands in contrast to the 'poverty of aspiration' thesis that is often referred to by politicians and even by practitioners in the field. However, more fine-grained distinctions in terms of cultural capital, which we will discuss later, may be relevant here.

While younger children from all backgrounds tend to have similar levels of aspiration, there needs to be further investigation and analysis of the mechanisms that moderate this aspiration over time. The Milburn Review of Access to the Professions (Milburn, 2009) presented some of the steps that could be taken to develop aspirations and translate them into improved outcomes. A key issue here is how expectations modify aspiration, particularly as students move through secondary school. Menzies (2013) found that disadvantaged pupils often have high aspirations, but they may not know how to achieve them and consequently may struggle to maintain them as a viable option. He also pointed to the importance of high-quality careers advice, work experience and work-related learning, together with learning-focused mentoring, in helping to maintain aspirations and expectations.

Thus, IAG is a key element of policy that is aimed at increasing participation both quantitatively and qualitatively, although it is also an area in which much more could be done. For example, recent work by the National Foundation for Educational Research (NFER) highlighted the lack of appropriately skilled and qualified careers staff in schools, with fewer than one in three of those delivering careers education having had any training in the area (McCrone *et al.*, 2009; see also Davies, 2012; Ofsted, 2013b). Such work highlights an important weakness in current provision in that, while one study found that many Year Seven students knew about university and said they wanted to go there, it also suggested that they had little idea about the steps they would need to follow to get there (Atherton *et al.*, 2009).

Bok (2010), using work carried out in Australia, argues that students from lower socio-economic backgrounds do have aspirations about going on to higher education, but 'have less developed capacities to realise them'. They therefore have 'to perform in a play *without a script*' (Bok, 2010: 175; emphasis in original). Despite their aspirations, they do not 'know the ropes', to use our own expression. Put another way, economic and cultural capital affect 'navigational capacity' (Appadurai, 2004: 69), which varies between those from different backgrounds. The ability to navigate educational pathways is also seen by Bok to be 'influenced by students' access to "hot" knowledge' provided by families and local networks (Bok, 2010: 176), with huge implications for those who are 'first in family', especially in terms of entry to 'elite' institutions. This analysis is somewhat reminiscent of Bernstein's discussion of those working-class families in the 1960s who valued the 'end' of having a grammar school education, but did not understand the 'means' of achieving it (Bernstein, 1977).

In similar terms, Menzies (2013) suggests that, in the current context in England, disadvantaged parents and people in their social networks can lack the experience and knowledge to help their children. He argues that engaging parents to help them understand what their children's aspirations involve and what will help them to achieve them is an effective way of raising attainment. It is, however, worth noting that other research has suggested that there do not seem to be any negative consequences associated with young people having high educational expectations, even if these are not realized (Reynolds and Baird, 2010).

Prior attainment

Regardless of these somewhat inconclusive findings about aspiration and expectations, it is clear that the major direct impediment to students proceeding to higher education is low prior attainment. Research undertaken at the Institute of Education, the London School of Economics and the Institute for Fiscal Studies

'Knowing the ropes'?

claims to have demonstrated this more clearly than ever before (Chowdry *et al.*, 2010). Since 2001 there has been a national census of all state school students, which collects information about individual students and allows us to track them through their schooling – thereby identifying which schools they attend and their performance in national tests. It also allows us to monitor the performance of different groups of students, including students who may receive Free School Meals (FSM) – the main proxy used by government to identify disadvantage. The research study, which was undertaken between 2005 and 2010, linked such census data to other data on which pupils entered higher education and which university they attended. Its headline finding was that, while there was a considerable gap in higher education participation between those from different backgrounds, this gap was actually very small once prior attainment had been fully taken into account. Figure 5.4 below shows the gap between men from different socio-economic backgrounds and how that gap disappears once prior academic attainment is controlled for. For women, too, the gap almost disappears.

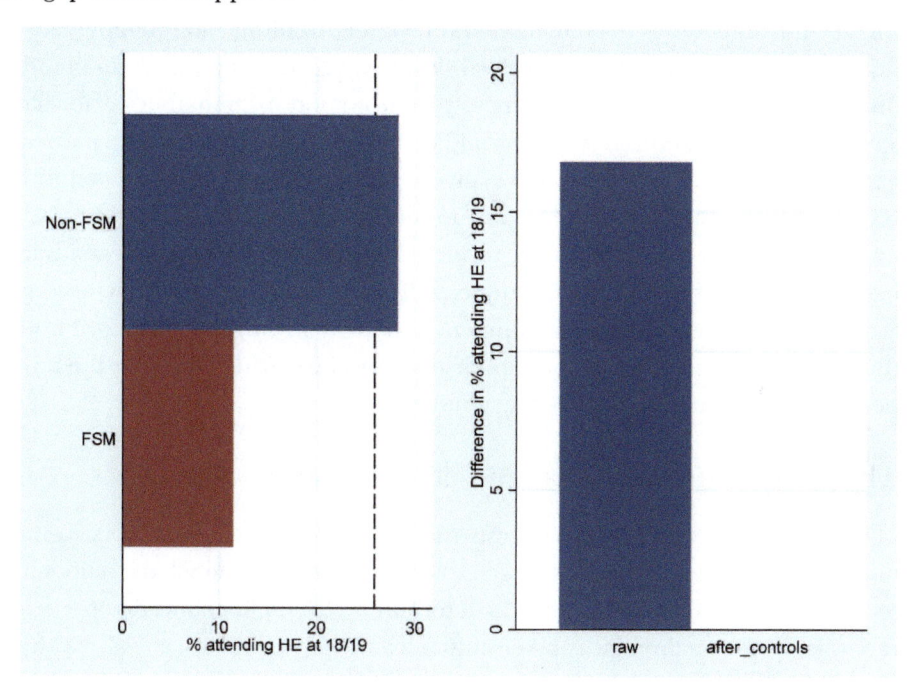

Figure 5.4: Raw socio-economic gap in higher education participation rates at age 18/19 for males (left-hand panel) and difference after adding in controls (right-hand panel)

Note: Dashed line is the average participation rate of all males.

Source: Vignoles and Crawford (2010).

Another finding of the research was that, while participation in 'high-status' universities was not evenly distributed across different groups when looking at the raw numbers, this bias towards higher socio-economic groups attending higher-status institutions was reduced once other variables were included. Again, it seems that prior attainment was driving the uneven distribution of students attending different types of higher education institutions, although the work by Boliver (2013) cited earlier suggests that this claim should be treated with caution at least in respect of some groups.

Nevertheless, Anders (2012) argues that much of the apparent socio-economic gradient in university participation can be accounted for by prior attainment as early as age 11. He finds little evidence of different success rates among university applicants with similar attainment at that age. As such, most of the participation gap arises at or before the decision to apply to university, with lower prior attainment by young people from more disadvantaged backgrounds preventing them from applying in the first place. Overall, this work concludes that socio-economic background per se does not have much of a direct impact on higher education entry. While participation and socio-economic background appear to be correlated, this relationship seems to be mediated through educational attainment.

A more recent study by Crawford (2014) suggests that the key school influence on participation may be its capacity to produce good examination performance at age 16. The implications from this would be that in order to narrow the participation gap, the only options likely to have any impact would be those targeted at raising school attainment for those from lower socio-economic backgrounds, and/or making use of contextual data to identify those students from less advantaged backgrounds, including those in underperforming schools, who may have greater academic potential than their attainment to date might suggest. Crawford notes that this latter approach seems to be supported by positive evidence about the university performance of such students once admitted.

The importance of social and cultural capital

Much of this research, then, suggests that – using standard indicators to measure disadvantage such as socio-economic group, student postcode or free school meals – social background is not important in determining the higher education participation rate once prior attainment is taken into account. Nevertheless, social disadvantage may prove to be a more significant influence if different indicators are used. Various studies have used other indicators, such as whether the family home is rented, the number of siblings, the books in the home and the level of education of the parents. It may therefore be that we need to consider students' social and cultural capital and not just their socio-economic status if we are to get a grip on patterns of participation. This argues for the use of sociological perspectives to complement the economic analyses that have dominated this area of work in recent years.

Cultural capital, as defined by Bourdieu, means culturally valued forms of privilege, specifically in terms of education and broader cultural taste, that are passed down through families and that, unlike money, do not take an overt economic form. Bourdieu believed that 'the transmission of cultural capital is no doubt the best hidden form of hereditary transmission of capital' (Bourdieu, 1986: 246). In studies of contemporary education systems, the concept of cultural capital is often used when considering how parents 'play' the education market (see, for example, Reay, 2004). The cultural capital acquired through a combination of well-informed, educated parents, high achieving schools and a peer group with similar aspirations and expectations tends to result in the higher attainment required to attend selective universities (Reay *et al.*, 2013). This particular combination of lifestyle, values, dispositions and expectations is often referred to in the sociological literature as a middle-class 'habitus', to use Bourdieu's own term.

Bourdieu's definition of social capital is less clear, but crucially includes access to durable social networks 'of more or less institutionalized relationships of mutual acquaintance and recognition', that can be drawn upon to perpetuate privilege (Bourdieu and Wacquant, 1992).[9] Families that lack past experience of higher education often find it difficult to provide the support and guidance their children need to make informed choices and do not have easy access to the sorts of networks that can help provide support and opportunities for middle-class families (Ball *et al.*, 2000; Reay *et al.*, 2005).

This does not mean that students from other backgrounds are entirely excluded even from high status universities, but we do need to bear in mind that the relatively small number of students from lower socio-economic groups attending the most prestigious universities means that they may well be untypical of their group in important respects that could remain even if attainment levels improve overall. Reay *et al.* (2009) interviewed high achievers from groups under-represented in higher education and found that, rather than feeling excluded, such students had developed the capacity to move between cultures. Their findings suggest that these students had embarked on this process early in their school careers, developing reflexivity and resilience that transformed their habitus.

Research undertaken for The Sutton Trust found that school students whose parents had not been to university were only likely to apply to the more prestigious universities if they were predicted to gain very high grades in their school leaving examinations. Conversely, students whose parents had attended university were more likely to apply to prestigious universities even with lower predicted grades (Curtis *et al.*, 2008). Shiner and Noden (2015) have recently confirmed that candidates from less privileged family backgrounds remain less likely to target high-status institutions even when other variables are taken into account. They note that self-exclusion by qualified candidates seemed to be a greater issue for low SES students than for black and minority ethnic candidates.

A small exploratory study by Noble and Davies (2009) sought to investigate empirically whether cultural capital influenced decision making about higher education. The researchers hypothesized that there may be cultural capital effects working independently of standard indicators of socio-economic factors, such as parental employment (although that does not necessarily mean independent of social class).[8] In order to test this hypothesis they constructed an instrument to measure the type of 'cultural capital' that appeared to result in successful progression to higher education and tested whether this had an impact – independent of parental background (as measured by occupation) and predicted grades – on the probability of a student's intention to participate in higher education. While this is obviously a different measure from whether they actually go, the research produced some interesting results. Predicted grades (used as the proxy for attainment) were still the most powerful predictor, but having the 'right' sort of cultural capital did appear to have an independent impact. The combination of lower attainment and the 'wrong' kind of cultural capital was particularly detrimental.

A later study by Davies *et al.* (2014) found a very strong association between parental education and intentions towards higher education and that cultural capital differences were more important to the choices of students expecting average grades than students expecting high grades. They also explored whether different aspects of cultural capital – indicated by engagement with 'highbrow culture', parent/school interaction and familiarity with current affairs – affected intentions, and found that each of their measures did have a positive impact. However, only the parent/school interaction element of cultural capital impacted on students' expectations of a graduate premium. The relevance of this is that students with high expectations of a graduate premium are more likely than others to want to go to university, after taking account of expected grades, home background, ethnicity and type of school attended. They hypothesize that one possible transmission mechanism is that students high in this aspect of cultural capital are able to access better information and this helps them to be more confident in their predictions of a graduate premium.

In the light of their findings, these researchers argue that it makes sense for widening participation initiatives to identify students with non-graduate parents, low levels of cultural capital or low graduate premium expectations as less likely than other students to intend to go to university. They suggest that awarding reduced fees or offering participation in outreach activities on the basis of income indicators at the personal level (e.g. eligibility for FSM) or the local level (e.g. area deprivation rates) seems less sensible than using indicators like these, which are more likely to be related to significantly lower intention to go to university.

Other work also suggests that the very process of deciding whether or not to go into higher education is significantly different for those from different cultural backgrounds. Ball *et al.* (2002) summarize two types of higher education 'chooser'.

The 'embedded chooser' is someone who is more likely than not to go on to higher education, whereas the 'contingent chooser' is less likely to progress on to higher education. Even though this categorization has its limitations, not least through being derived from a comparison between individuals with multiple differences, it is useful heuristically. If more contingent choosers are to enter higher education, an area that is particularly important is the support, advice, guidance and encouragement given to students, usually through their schools, in applying to university – including choice of course and institution. Unfortunately, as indicated earlier, existing arrangements here leave much to be desired (Davies, 2012) and recent changes may even have exacerbated the problem. In particular, such provision is vital for those young people whose family does not possess relevant cultural capital and social networks to provide appropriate support and guidance.

With regard to qualitative inequality in particular, Demack *et al.* (2012), using data from the Longitudinal Study of Young People in England (LSYPE), found that young people engaging with activities 'culturally valued' within a middle class habitus were much more likely to access Russell Group universities than their peers, although the relationship was largely indirect. Davies *et al.* (2014) point out that cultural capital may play a role in admissions to elite universities that is different from the role it plays in the choice of whether to go to college at all. Work on admissions to Oxford by Zimdars *et al.* (2009) has provided some insights into this. Adapting their own measure of cultural capital to suit 'a highly competitive educational transition', they found that it was not just participation in activities associated with 'high culture', such as playing a musical instrument or visiting museums, that counted in that context. Rather, they concluded, 'children who read and understand high culture … fare particularly well in the competition for a place at Oxford' (Zimdars *et al.*, 2009: 661).

School as well as parental background may be particularly relevant here. Some research by BIS and The Sutton Trust (BIS, 2009c) examined where the barriers lay in terms of students from different types of schools attending what they regarded as the more prestigious institutions. This showed that, while there were significant differences between the proportions of similarly qualified students attending prestigious institutions from different types of schools, this seemed to be due to disparities in applications to these types of institutions rather than any bias from admissions tutors at the point of entry. Mangan *et al.* (2010) identify a big difference between private and state schools in the support they offer students, so that the former actively reinforce the already strong expectation that their students will attend this type of university (Riddell, 2010). This suggests that even more support is needed at state schools and colleges if their students are to consider applying to more selective universities.

This may seem to shift responsibility away from the universities and admissions tutors who are often charged with presenting barriers to higher education participation. However, other research suggests that cultural practices and processes within institutions do still have an effect on admissions, as even a standard 'fair access' approach tends to favour those with a particular sort of cultural capital. In their work on admissions to Fine Art degrees, Burke and McManus (2009) certainly uncovered a range of unintended exclusionary practices within contemporary admissions processes.

Two projects undertaken at the IOE for The Sutton Trust are also relevant here. One project examined the effectiveness and sustainability of relationships between schools and universities (Tough *et al.*, 2008) and advocated more work with younger children; more sustained interventions engaging the whole cohort, not just a select group; more joint working between teachers and university staff, especially on activities around academic subjects; and involving parents where possible. The project by Curtis *et al.* (2008) mentioned earlier looked specifically at the support and advice given in schools around applying to the more prestigious universities. It found that, even in schools that had a good track record of sending relatively high proportions of pupils to such universities despite a relatively disadvantaged intake, there was a lack of systematic discussion about the status of universities and a hesitancy to encourage borderline students to apply to the 'Sutton 13' institutions. In fact, teachers were wary of students 'over-aspiring' and tried to make them be more 'realistic'. The project recommended that schools should ensure that their pupils know about the full spectrum of universities, that school staff should be open with pupils regarding the characteristics of different universities and that universities should be more transparent about their admissions policies.

Finally, it is important to note that cultural capital and type of schooling are important in decisions about courses as well as those about institutions. As Coyne and Goodfellow (2008) note, choices made in terms of future study at ages 14 and 16 determine both the level of Science, Technology, Engineering and Mathematics (STEM) skills in the population and also the numbers of students with the necessary background to continue studying STEM subjects post-16 and at university level. Archer *et al.* (2012) point to the role of family background in such decisions about which subjects to study. Archer (2013: 13) uses the concept of 'science capital' to mean 'science-related qualifications, understanding, knowledge (about science and 'how it works'), as well as interest and social contacts (e.g. knowing someone who works in a science-related job)'. She reported that, by Year 9, only 32 per cent of those with 'low science capital' had career aspirations in STEM subjects, as compared with 60 per cent of those with 'high science capital'. Such findings suggest that targeting of widening participation outreach activities should focus on those without relevant aspects of the middle-class habitus described above (rather than being entirely led by the HEFCE benchmarks of socio-economic class and low-participation neighbourhoods), and that outreach activities themselves should provide subject enhancement opportunities to develop 'subject capital', as described by Archer in relation to science.

However, the role of schools themselves in the reproduction of patterns of subject choice is again significant. Harris (2010: 73) observed that one has only to recognize that 'the range of sciences offered in independent and selective schools is often wider (than in non-selective state schools), and that science-based subjects such as medicine are disproportionately offered by selective universities and at least some of the reasons for a skewed application pool are immediately very clear'.

It seems then that some quite complex interactions between home, school and university cultures pose a considerable challenge for those seeking to widen participation and fair access in higher education and these help to explain why only limited progress has been made to date.

Future directions

We have shown that, while some progress has been made in increasing the proportion of the population experiencing higher education, there is still a considerable way to go in widening participation. Significant issues remain, particularly in relation to achieving entry to more selective universities for those from lower socio-economic backgrounds and especially those with limited access to the sorts of social and cultural capital that facilitate entry to higher education.

Even when disadvantaged young people do enter higher education, they are more likely to drop out. Vignoles and Powdthavee (2009) found that, even when prior attainment and other individual characteristics were taken into account, there was a significant gap in the rate of dropout by the end of the first year at university, suggesting that retention is at least as important as are barriers at the point of entry to higher education in terms of equity. The new National Strategy for Access and Student Success (BIS, 2014), with its emphasis on the student lifecycle, should help to move this issue up the agenda. There has already been some research exploring why people drop out (e.g. Johnes and McNabb, 2004), as well as examining the experiences of non-traditional groups at university, including the pedagogies and teaching styles used and the kinds of support and advice available to them (e.g. Crozier *et al.*, 2008). Universities need to engage fully with the issues around transition, retention and student success that affect the trajectories of those from under-represented groups.

In terms of employability and future careers we have to recognize that, even with wider participation in undergraduate education, social advantage may also be gained from the differential opportunities universities offer for students to have 'more than just a degree'. As Bathmaker *et al.* (2013: 741) argue, 'when the playing field appears to have been levelled for some people ... advantage is maintained through a shift in the rules of the game', an example perhaps of the aforementioned 'Effectively Maintained Inequality' and similar to the case of the moving goalposts in school examinations discussed in Chapter 4.

It is likely that the key battleground for widening participation and fair access to elite occupations will increasingly shift to postgraduate and post-graduation experience (Whitty and Mullan, 2013). Universities are beginning to recognize this as a real issue for poorer students who are relying on their degrees to gain access to the graduate labour market. Institutions need to develop a range of targeted interventions and curriculum-related activities to ensure that undergraduate students from under-represented groups can benefit from the opportunities for placements, work experience, careers advice and links with leading employers that are available to more privileged students through their existing networks. Indicators of increases in students' social capital and social agency being piloted by HEFCE (2014b) may help to give this greater priority.

Yet it is clear that only limited progress can be made without more substantial social and cultural changes in the world beyond education. Even if disadvantaged students successfully negotiate entry to the professions, they can face new barriers on entering employment. For example, there have been two recent reports that suggest that graduates from disadvantaged backgrounds face hurdles in employment when compared with their more advantaged peers, despite performing equally well at university. Laurison and Friedman (2015) provide evidence that upwardly mobile graduates entering elite occupations often face difficulties in progressing within those occupations. Similarly, Anders (2015) finds that private-school-educated entrants to high-status occupations have faster pay progression than state school entrants, even allowing for such factors as the type of university attended. And alongside this 'class ceiling', as Laurison and Friedman call it, there may be a 'glass floor' by which more advantaged families are able to protect their offspring from downward mobility, as even low-achieving children from such backgrounds seem to benefit in the labour market from their parents' higher levels of education (McKnight, 2015).

This means that writers like Burke (2012) and Gale (2015) are undoubtedly right that widening participation needs to be reconceptualized as a project of social justice in the widest sense. Yet, at least until the very recent election of Jeremy Corbyn as leader of the Labour Party, there has been little, if any, appetite among the main political parties for radical redistributive policies. However, that does not mean that we should abandon the struggle for social justice in and through education, merely that (as we saw in the case of schools) we have to be realistic about what can be achieved through higher education initiatives alone. At the very least, it is important to protect the gains that have already been made, especially as there have been suggestions that we are now experiencing 'a retreat from widening participation' (McCaig, 2016: 215).

There are also some actions that might be taken within existing policy frameworks to encourage more individuals from non-traditional backgrounds to consider entry to all forms of higher education and acquire the means to do so especially through knowing the ropes. These include a continuing focus on narrowing attainment gaps and supporting aspiration much earlier in pupils' educational careers; radically improving the quality of information, advice and guidance that young people receive about higher education and its different forms; ensuring that school–university links are developed for all schools; and undertaking joint activities on a more regular basis than has been the case in many universities. In addition, funding for carefully targeted mentoring, including academic mentoring, needs to be provided to keep young people in education longer and to support students from non-traditional backgrounds through higher education, while parents and communities need to be more fully involved in universities' outreach activities. And, for the time being anyway, contextual data about student backgrounds should be used as part of the toolbox for making admissions decisions, especially at highly selective universities.[10]

Although Gale and Hodge (2014) are correct to point to the limitations of incremental change along such lines, reflexive engagements with policies and practices in widening participation have the potential to illuminate underlying cultural and economic inequalities, as demonstrated in this chapter. Furthermore, having a wider cross-section of the population engaged in higher education with the capacity to contest prevailing discourses may itself be a significant driver of cultural change. The alternative is that universities, and especially elite universities, continue to serve mainly those from higher socio-economic groups, to the detriment of the academy, society as whole and especially those from under-represented groups who will remain excluded from higher education and the opportunities it offers.

We also need greater numbers of alternative and critical perspectives that highlight and problematize the many aspects of the system that widening participation activities themselves typically leave unquestioned (Southgate and Bennett, 2014). However, while post-structural research on education policy has been strong on deconstruction and critique, it has too rarely recognized 'the requirement for there to be identifiable structures, institutions and minimal consensus ... for any viable politics to occur' (Gulson and Metcalfe, 2015: 3). Indeed, it sometimes questions that requirement itself. As a result, in calling for new imaginaries, it does little to address the likely barriers to realizing these new imaginaries, other than at a symbolic level. In the higher education context, knowledges and pedagogies currently excluded from or marginalized in the academy certainly need to be given greater prominence, as sociologists of educational knowledge have been arguing for years. But the development of meaningful alternatives to conventional university education, as advocated by its critics, will take time and face resistance. We should surely not accept that in the meantime certain groups will be effectively excluded from higher education. We thus need to improve access to what exists *and* change what people gain access to. In our view, social justice demands both.

Notes

[1] 'Old' universities are those that were part of the university sector prior to 1992, while 'new' universities refers to those higher education institutions that received university status after 1992. The pattern is reversed for those from lower social classes, with 21 per cent of entrants to new universities and 14 per cent of entrants to old universities coming from 'skilled manual' families. These percentages are calculated from UCAS data of all full-time entrants to higher education in 2001/2 (Boliver, 2008).

[2] The 'Sutton 13' list of universities identified those HEIs ranked most highly in an average of published university league tables, namely Birmingham, Bristol, Cambridge, Durham, Edinburgh, Imperial College, London School of Economics, Nottingham, Oxford, St Andrews, University College London, Warwick and York (BIS, 2009c).

[3] In this study, 'high status' universities were defined as the (then) 20 members of the Russell Group, together with 21 other institutions whose score in the 2008 Research Assessment Exercise matched or exceeded that of the lowest-scoring member of the Russell Group.

[4] OFFA classifies institutions according to whether, relative to other institutions, they subject their young entrants to higher, medium or lower points tariffs for entry, where points are awarded for qualifications.

[5] This has perhaps been reflected in the A-level entry statistics for 2015 (Sellgren, 2015).

[6] In some ways, this is little different from the post-recession position of the New Labour Government (BIS, 2009a) or of the Labour Party in opposition (Miliband, 2014).

[7] As this book was going to press, the incoming Conservative Government was expected to issue a Green Paper about the future of higher education, including proposals for a Teaching Excellence Framework (TEF). The expectation was that any increases in fee levels beyond those linked to inflation would be dependent on an institution's performance in the TEF.

[8] Social relationships and networks are also key features of other sociological conceptualizations of social capital, even though they are grounded in different theoretical traditions and empirical circumstances (Coleman, 1988; Putnam, 2001).

[9] Harrison and Waller (2010) have criticized the way in which the concept of cultural capital is used in the research by Davies and colleagues, and particularly what they regard as an implication that it is independent of social class.

[10] About 15 years ago, I wrote a thinkpiece called 'Who shall have prizes?', in which I suggested that university admissions tutors should consider making lower offers to students in the light of the circumstances under which they were studying. I got more abusive responses to that article than I had had at any time since, as an 18-year-old, I had written to my local paper attacking the policies of the National Front. Recently, however, the use of contextual data in decisions about admissions has gained considerable traction and, as this book goes to press, the Social Mobility and Child Poverty Commission was expected to endorse this approach in its 2015 annual report.

Chapter 6
The continuing importance of the sociology of education

Introduction

Soon after I was appointed as Director of the Institute of Education in 2000, someone referred to me as 'Geoff Whitty, who used to be a sociologist of education', and I have to admit that there were times during my ten-year tenure as Director when I was distracted from sociology of education by administrative and financial preoccupations, and other times when I felt distinctly out of step with the directions my discipline was taking.[1] However, I have always seen my primary academic and professional identity as a sociologist of education, and continue to do so, although strictly speaking I only studied sociology officially as a postgraduate student and, formally, I had the word 'sociology' in my job title only when I succeeded Basil Bernstein – of whom more later – in the role of Karl Mannheim Professor of Sociology of Education at the IOE in 1992. Nevertheless, in this final chapter, I want to reaffirm the importance of sociology of education, first of all in my own professional life as a teacher and academic committed to the pursuit of social justice, and then as an essential tool in making sense of contemporary education policy and particularly in helping us to understand the contexts in which policy is made and enacted.

My life with the sociology of education

For about nine months before I went up to Cambridge to study history in 1965, at the age of 18, I was a temporary teacher at an inner-city primary school in west London. It was a time when the area was experiencing significant immigration by families from the British Commonwealth, mainly from the Caribbean, the Indian sub-continent and parts of Africa. The area also had a longstanding white working-class population with low educational attainment. Interestingly, the area now has long since been gentrified, and is nowadays among the most expensive areas of London to live in. But at the time it exposed me to lots of experiences that had been unknown to me growing up in the outer suburbs of London. In particular it forced me to confront and question a lot of my taken-for-granted assumptions, especially those that informed my own schooling at a selective grammar school.

It also turned me against the elitist educational environment I was about to enter at Cambridge and I spent, as was not uncommon in the 1960s, most of my time as a student activist protesting against everything from the Vietnam War to my college's ban on overnight guests of the opposite sex (see Linehan, 2011). I did not spend anything like as much time on the history and political theory I was supposed to be studying, apart from that which was directly relevant to my political activities. Much of that was Marxist literature but, early on in my time at Cambridge, I was also involved in a Fabian Society study group that exposed me to the sociology of education for the first time, in particular to work that is usually called the 'political arithmetic tradition' in Britain, an approach that studies the relationship between social background and educational achievement, largely in quantitative terms (e.g. Floud *et al.*, 1956). As I indicate later, such work dominated our field in Britain in the early 1960s. Even though it was very different from much of the Marxist literature I was also reading, political arithmetic's identification of school drop-out as both an economic and a social justice issue convinced me that sociological studies of education – including the mapping of inequalities by class in particular, but also race and gender – could be an important educational and political resource.[2]

When I left Cambridge in 1968, I trained as a history and social studies teacher at the London Institute of Education and then became a secondary school teacher, not far from where I had been an unqualified temporary teacher a few years earlier. Although I was one of a generation whose student activism was thus superseded in employment by a 'long march through the institutions', I increasingly felt the need to understand why the change that was so obviously needed in overcoming embedded inequalities was so difficult to achieve. I discussed this experience some years later in the preface to *Sociology and School Knowledge* (Whitty, 1985). I was reminded of it recently when a statement I made there about the grammar school curriculum being 'meaningless' to many of the working-class pupils I was teaching was attacked by Christodoulou (2013), a neo-conservative member of the academy school movement, as feeding a dangerous progressive myth that teaching knowledge is (middle-class) indoctrination and therefore to be avoided.[3]

Ironically, I had turned to a serious study of the sociology of education to avoid such simplistic analyses, even though I was soon to find they often thrived within the discipline itself. I wanted sociology to help me understand not only why change was so difficult but also what strategies of change might be feasible, whether at an individual, institutional or societal level. So, in the early 1970s, I returned to the IOE to undertake postgraduate studies in the sociology of education, being taught by some of the leading figures in the field in England at that time, such as Basil Bernstein and Michael F. D. Young, both of whom I had already encountered and been inspired by when I had trained as a teacher there a few years earlier.

The 'old' and 'new' sociologies of education

When I started studying sociology of education in earnest, I discovered that I had been born days before the untimely death in January 1947 of Karl Mannheim, whom some would consider the founding father of sociology of education in Britain. Even though we could not be said to be members of the same 'generation unit', to use one of his more enduring concepts, there are some aspects of his approach to the subject that have always appealed to me more than those of some of my closer contemporaries. His dual commitment to theory and policy prefigured my own, and I could identify with his struggles with relativism within the sociology of knowledge and with his difficulties in demonstrating the connections between his theoretical work and his policy prescriptions. It was therefore fitting that Karl Mannheim himself would subsequently be the subject of a commemorative professorial lecture I delivered as Karl Mannheim Professor at the Institute in 1997 (Whitty, 1997).

Educational sociology had already been developing in the UK before the Second World War, but it was arguably the appointment in 1946 of Mannheim, a leading European social theorist who had left Germany in the 1930s, to a Chair of Education at what was then called the University of London Institute of Education that established the sub-discipline of sociology of education within English academia. Although Mannheim himself did not publish much specifically on the subject in his lifetime, his lectures and notes in this field were published posthumously in 1962 by his student W. A. Campbell Stewart as *An Introduction to the Sociology of Education* (Mannheim and Stewart, 1962). This was staple reading on the subject when I first became familiar with it in the mid-1960s, but it did not define the field for long and I never found its substantive, often social psychological, content particularly compelling.

But even in the 1950s, the sociology of education had begun to take a rather different path in Britain. Among its leading exponents was Jean Floud, Reader in the Sociology of Education at the Institute of Education, who had known Mannheim at the London School of Economics. Floud's own work lacked the theoretical sweep that characterized Mannheim's, and she explicitly rejected what she saw as his heavy-handed approach to post-war social and educational planning (Floud, 1959). Instead, Floud was linked to the 'political arithmetic tradition' of studies on social class and educational achievement (Floud *et al.*, 1956; Halsey *et al.*, 1961) that I mentioned earlier. This was the work that first led me into the sociology of education as a member of that Fabian Society study group in Cambridge. Political arithmetic's focus on 'early leaving' and 'wastage of talent' influenced the Labour Party in its espousal of comprehensive secondary education, and this apparent link between academic work and political action excited me. As Olive Banks – whose textbook on the subject (Banks, 1968) soon superseded Mannheim and Stewart's – said of the political arithmetic tradition, there were 'some grounds for thinking that the sociology of education has changed to some extent the policymakers' way of thinking about educational issues' (Banks, 1974: 6).

One of Floud's successors as Reader in the Sociology of Education at the IOE was Basil Bernstein. Described by Banks (1974: 5) as 'perhaps the most eminent of the sociologists to work in this field', he took its study at the Institute back into the realm of social theory via his socio-linguistic studies of class differences in children's language (Bernstein, 1971). While his own work was firmly located in the Durkheimian tradition, the established Chair to which he was subsequently appointed was called the Karl Mannheim Chair of the Sociology of Education, and this was the Chair that I later held and that was until recently held by Stephen Ball, whose work has been cited a number of times in this book.

As it happens, I studied at the Institute just at the time when its sociologists, led by Michael F. D. Young, whom Bernstein recruited to the Institute in 1967 and whose student I became, were producing the ground-breaking edited collection called *Knowledge and Control* (Young, 1971). This heralded 'new directions for the sociology of education', which were self-consciously distinguished from the 'old' sociology of education of Floud, Halsey and their colleagues. This work was becoming dominant at the Institute when I studied the subject there in the late 1960s and early 1970s and, to some extent, my own contribution was identified with this 'new' sociology of education when I was teaching at the University of Bath in the 1970s.

Yet I would contend that both the 'old' and the 'new' sociology of education – along with studies from the Manchester School, like Hargreaves (1967) and Lacey (1970), which also influenced me as a student and as a teacher – had a common theme that brought me into the subject then and continues to motivate me today. Despite its various turns and brief forays into other issues, the sociology of education in England has always been centrally (but by no means exclusively, of course) concerned with the differential performance of middle-class and working-class students in the education system. That is also an issue that has influenced virtually all the policies I have discussed earlier in this book.

As I have described elsewhere (Whitty, 1985), I saw the 'old' sociology of education of the 1950s and 1960s as largely concerned with mapping social inequalities in education or exploring how the cultural features of working-class homes and communities militated against the success in school of children from such backgrounds (Craft, 1970). Its policy focus was therefore on how those 'deficits' might be compensated, in order that children from such backgrounds could succeed. While the school system, and particularly its selective nature, was seen to be implicated in this wastage of talent, relatively little attention was paid to the content of schooling itself. In many of the studies at that time, there was a confident assumption that what they took for granted as education was a worthwhile 'good' in itself, and that it was in the interests of both individuals and the national economy that they should receive more of it. In other words, the key issue was access to schooling.

The 'new' sociology of education rather reversed the argument. It suggested that the crucial determinant of who succeeded and who failed was the nature of what they encountered in school and that it was therefore hardly surprising that middle-class children succeeded, because they understood the culture of the school, which was essentially consonant with their own. This seemed to justify various forms of 'progressive' or 'child-centred' pedagogy or alternative curricula closer to the experience of working-class children, in the terms of which they could succeed. I characterized this approach at the time as 'naïve possibilitarianism' (Whitty, 1974). For me, it failed to recognize that, although the curriculum as it existed was but one of a number of possibilities, each of which might interact differently with the culture of the home, its dominant form served particular social functions that might not be so easily overturned.

Similar arguments were put forward by Sharp and Green (1975), and by the late 1970s the second phase of the so-called 'new' sociology of education in England came to be dominated by neo-Marxist approaches influenced by the American writers Bowles and Gintis (1976). In complete contrast to the possibilitarianism of the earlier phase, much of this neo-Marxist work seemed to deny any real possibility of change from within the education system, whose nature was seen as structurally determined by the needs of the capitalist economy. It seemed that everyday professional practices, even if carried out by well-meaning professionals, merely sustained broader structures of oppression whose origins lay elsewhere. Ethnographic studies of everyday practices in schools and classrooms at this time were sometimes rather less pessimistic, but even pupil agency was often seen to contribute to social and cultural reproduction, as writers like Willis (1977) and Corrigan (1979) demonstrated how working-class pupils actively participated in their own positioning in the class structure.

Both phases of the 'new' sociology of education were seen as dangerous by the New Right critics mentioned in Chapter 2, particularly in terms of their potential impact on teachers. An Open University course on *Schooling and Society* came in for particular criticism in this respect (Gould, 1977), and my own association with it was raised as an issue in the interview for my lectureship at King's College London in 1980. At about the same time, Dawson (1981: 60) argued that the sociology of education, initially 'ineffectual' but no longer 'harmless', should 'be cut out of courses for student teachers ... to improve the intellectual and moral environment in which would-be teachers are taught'. However, in reality, the influence of the sociology of education on policy and practice at that time was probably much less significant than either its advocates hoped or its critics feared.

The sociology of education policy

Michael Young has rightly pointed out to me that our own joint work at that time (Whitty and Young, 1976; Young and Whitty, 1977) does not fit neatly into either the possibilitarian or the deterministic approaches characterized above. This is perhaps one of the reasons why my own substantive interest shifted somewhat in the 1980s towards education policy and into empirical studies of education policymaking. One particular interest was the role of private schooling in English education, which I pursued with my old school history teacher, Tony Edwards (Edwards *et al.*, 1989), who had himself by then become a leading scholar in the sociology of education (Edwards, 1976).

During this period, English education became increasingly overtly politicized. Elected in 1979, Margaret Thatcher's Conservative Government introduced neo-conservative policies of state control and prescription in relation to the National Curriculum and national assessment, while also encouraging neo-liberal market forces through parental choice and school autonomy. Another aspect of our work during these years was trying to make sense of these apparently contradictory developments in sociological terms (Whitty, 1989; Whitty *et al.*, 1998).

The sociology of education in Britain became increasingly dominated by the sociology of education policy at this time and I was by no means the only sociologist of education who took this route. Although it had already been a feature of the work I myself had undertaken at King's College London in the early 1980s, the sociology of education policy soon came to be identified with a group that grew up around my successor there, Stephen Ball. Another group joined me at Bristol Polytechnic, where I headed up the Education faculty in the second part of that decade.

Within this work the longstanding focus in British sociology of education on what is usually regarded as 'working-class failure' remained evident, although the way of approaching it was now via an attempt to understand how education policy, whatever its claims, has in practice consistently favoured middle-class children (see, for example, Power *et al.*, 2003; Ball, 2003; Reay, 2008). In some ways, this was rather less novel than we sometimes claimed (Power and Whitty, 2006), as this phenomenon was central to what had been demonstrated by the political arithmetic tradition (Halsey *et al.*, 1980). Ball (2011a: 960) has similarly pointed out that *Education and the Working Class* (Jackson and Marsden, 1962) 'anticipated Bourdieu's point that we need a theory of advantage as well as disadvantage'. What was perhaps more novel at this time was the emphasis, particularly by Ball himself and his colleagues, on middle-class strategies for maintaining their advantage.

Even so, as Young has pointed out, the debate between the 'old' and the 'new' sociologies, 'which seemed all-important to many of us at the time', was in large part 'an example of generational conflict within the academic community' (Young, 2008a: 220). I guess the same might be said of the lack of enthusiasm on some of our parts for the post-modernist perspectives that had gained currency within the sociology of education, particularly since the 1990s (Hill *et al.*, 2002). It may also be, as Young hints, that the 'extreme relativism' of those perspectives reminded some of us of the shortcomings of the first phase of the 'new' sociology of education.

Return to the knowledge question

As we have seen, Tony Blair's New Labour Government, first elected in 1997, emphasized policies of parental choice and school diversity as the key to educational improvement and closing the social class attainment gap (Whitty, 2008; Whitty, 2009). The Coalition Government elected in 2010 continued this trend with its policies on academies and free schools. However, more traditional Conservative policies also experienced a revival at that time, and the nature of school knowledge was put firmly back onto the policy agenda. Michael Gove, as Secretary of State for Education from 2010 to 2014, took the view that what working-class children needed to succeed was exposure to the traditional curriculum. His so-called English Baccalaureate reinforced the role of traditional subjects in the curriculum, as we saw in Chapter 4, and reflected his belief that it was an indictment of recent educational history 'that just around 16 per cent manage to succeed in getting to secure a C pass or better at GCSE in English, Maths, the sciences, a language and history or geography' (Gove, 2011). A whole series of other reforms to school examinations sought to roll back any tendency towards a skills-based curriculum and 'progressive' approaches to teaching and assessment.[4]

In a lecture while in opposition, Gove had cited the Italian Marxist Antonio Gramsci to support his view that educational methods that called themselves 'progressive' were actually regressive in social terms. He argued that 'with the abandonment of subject disciplines, the poorer lose out ... Richer parents who can afford it access specific subject teaching earlier rather than later with the most successful prep schools introducing discrete subjects taught by subject specialists before pupils go on to secondary education' (Gove, 2008). Not surprisingly, Gove was also an admirer of E. D. Hirsch and the work of his Core Knowledge Foundation (Hirsch, 1999).

Meanwhile, the sociology of education itself went back to the 'knowledge question', but in very different terms from those it had employed in the 1970s. In particular, my colleague Michael F. D. Young, whose earlier work had been seen as supportive of progressive approaches to education, now distanced himself from such an interpretation of his position. He questioned whether subject-based curricula only favoured middle-class children and suggested that project- or theme-based curricula, which had been thought to better suit working-class children, were even more socially regressive. Thus, Young's *Bringing Knowledge Back In* (Young, 2008a) was a critique of progressivism and constructivism, and indeed of the 'new' sociology of education itself, at least as powerful as any offered by Conservative politicians, although his more recent work has also identified the limitations of Conservative ministers' position on the curriculum (Young, 2011). Even so, Young's apparent volte-face has been warmly welcomed by neo-conservative critics of progressive education such as Christodoulou (2013).

Young now considers that the distinctive role of schools is to transmit knowledge. While his earlier work critiqued what counted as knowledge and who had access to it, he now stresses the necessity of what he calls 'powerful knowledge', as this is the knowledge needed to progress in the world (Young, 2009). He argues that 'the everyday local knowledge that pupils bring to school ... can never be the basis for the curriculum [because] it cannot provide the basis for any generalisable principles' (Young, 2009: 16). He further suggests that 'powerful' knowledge is especially important for working-class pupils who do not have access to it at home, arguing that 'the knowledge issue is both an epistemological issue and a social justice issue' (Young, 2008b: para. 6). He is therefore concerned that some apparently progressive curricular offers open to such pupils, including too many vocational courses, lack both substance and currency.

I have sometimes teased Young by pointing out that his current position is not only rather close to that of some neo-conservatives but also (and this is perhaps more palatable to him) reminiscent of the arguments put by two of the groups who were his major antagonists when I was a student of his in the 1970s. At one level it appears similar to the position of philosophers like Paul Hirst (1969), who then argued for a curriculum based on 'forms of knowledge', either for epistemological reasons or because in a stratified society there are principled and expedient reasons for giving all pupils access to high-status knowledge. Young also now seems much closer to the materialist critics of the 'relativism' associated with the phenomenological version of the new sociology of education that emerged from his early work (Young, 1971). The Marxist historian Brian Simon (1976), for example, feared that its relativist ideological position would deny the working class access to knowledge, culture and science, a criticism that troubled me at the time, if not too many of my contemporaries in Young's classes at the Institute.

The continuing relevance of Basil Bernstein

The sociologist whose work, in my view, remains most helpful in thinking through the relationship between social class and school knowledge is Bernstein, who remained the dominant presence within the sociology of education in the UK until his death in 2000 and indeed beyond. I can date my own first exposure to Bernstein to a lecture at the Institute on 11 October 1968, when I was training to be a teacher. Basil inspired me far more than anyone had succeeded in doing during my undergraduate degree at Cambridge and he has been a pervasive influence on my own academic life ever since. I can still conjure up in my mind his words, his presence on the stage and his mannerisms while delivering his lectures. And, although over the years I have struggled with the depth and richness of many of his more difficult concepts and ideas, it was actually a very simple statement on that particular day in 1968 that was the 'road to Damascus' moment that turned me into a sociologist of the curriculum.

The continuing importance of the sociology of education

Before Basil's lecture that day there would have been another contribution, from a philosopher, probably on education as an intrinsically worthwhile activity or on forms of knowledge as the basis for the curriculum, but I have no recollection of either the form or the content of that contribution. Then it was Basil's turn. Coming to the front of the stage, he said, 'Just for a moment forget what you've just heard and forget what is actually in the school curriculum you're going to teach year in year out for the next however many years. Just think of it as a series of empty units of time spread through the week. Then ask yourselves why and how some things come to fill up those units and not others. Why' – he said, in a characteristic aside – 'is poetry in there and not pornography? And why do some subjects, like maths, get all the good slots, while general studies gets left with the dregs on Friday afternoons? And why are some subjects kept apart with strong barriers between them and others allowed to permeate each other in time and space?' I was soon to realize the potency of this simple idea, which can now be seen to have informed much of the subsequent British work in the sociology of the school curriculum (Bernstein, 1977; Young, 1971; Whitty, 1985).

Bernstein died just three weeks into my Directorship of the Institute, and both the Institute and the field knew they had lost their greatest contemporary scholar (Power *et al.*, 2001). Significantly, Young himself now resorts to Bernstein – with whom he had 'differences' in later years (Young, 2008a: 220) – in support of his own current approach to the curriculum. I, too, have returned to Bernstein's work in recent years. As I have argued at greater length elsewhere (Whitty, 2010a), some of his key concepts help explain why it has proved so difficult for working-class children to succeed in English schools and also to clarify enduring issues about the role of curriculum and pedagogy in educational success and failure (Bernstein, 1977). In my view, his work is thus highly relevant to contemporary policy and curricular issues.

In his comments on 'compensatory education', Bernstein (1971) certainly suggested that schools needed to take into account children's experience in the family and community. However, he recognized that the idea that simply weakening boundaries between home and school would of itself make a significant difference was both empirically and theoretically difficult to sustain. His later work on knowledge structures questioned both the possibility and the desirability of collapsing such boundaries (Bernstein, 1996). Even in an early article, he argued that education must involve the introduction of children to the universalistic meanings of public forms of thought (Bernstein, 1970). So, while Bernstein sometimes urged teachers to forge greater connections between school knowledge and everyday knowledge, I suspect that, despite some ambiguity in one of his papers, this was more a pedagogic than an epistemological point.

In the present debates about the school curriculum, I would imagine that Bernstein would have argued that all children should have access to high-status knowledge but might get there by different means. He would probably have supported the kind of approach recommended by Fantini and Weinstein (1968: 347) in the 1960s, who argued that 'a curriculum for the disadvantaged must begin as closely as possible to the pupils' direct experience' because 'without such an approach, the abstract cannot be attained'. This is very different from the position of writers like Nell Keddie, who rejected the idea that home culture might be used as a 'bridge' into mainstream culture and 'bodies of knowledge', as this would be unnecessary if, as some relativists claimed, 'all cultures – class and ethnic – [had] their own logics which [were] capable of grappling with ... abstract thought' (Keddie, 1973: 18).

Unfortunately, it is the latter position that politicians still use to deny the value of sociological perspectives on education, a stance that may also be encouraged by some postmodernist writings in our field (see Apple, 1993). More generally, as Beck (2012) has pointed out, Michael Gove's passion when Secretary of State for the teaching of the 'traditional' disciplines in schools was not matched by any enthusiasm for the inclusion of 'education disciplines' like the sociology of education in teacher training. Our work was once again regarded as 'ideologically suspect' and part of a conspiracy on the part of the 'educational establishment' (which he called 'the Blob') to excuse failure and deny the working classes a proper education (Whitty, 2014).

Although it is often disregarded on the grounds of the difficulty of its language, Bernstein's work would nevertheless bear careful study by Michael Gove and his likes, not least because Gove himself argues that 'the greatest pleasures are those which need to be worked at' (Gove, 2011). He would find that Bernstein's work demonstrates the intractability of the relationship between knowledge, schooling and inequality, but also provides a way of thinking about what would need to be put in place if that relationship were to be interrupted. Of course education cannot, as Bernstein (1970) himself noted, compensate for society in any simple way, but that does not mean that educators should accept the continuing failure of the disadvantaged as inevitable. Some of the key challenges in giving disadvantaged pupils access to powerful knowledge – and giving them meaningful and critical purchase on their everyday lives – are pedagogic rather than curricular. And, even though it may not offer politicians simplistic policy prescriptions, Bernstein's work identifies key issues and gives us resources for thinking through what needs to be done, as does other work on social and cultural reproduction discussed in Chapters 4 and 5 (e.g. Bourdieu and Passeron, 1977).

Sociology and education policy today

Social class inequalities in education have been an enduring policy theme in English education since the early part of the twentieth century and, as I have argued here, they have also been the predominant theme of the sociology of education. So, if there is both theoretical and empirical work relevant to the key policy issues of today, why is sociology of education not in greater evidence in current debates about social class attainment and participation gaps in English education? After all, one of my predecessors as Director of the Institute, Sir Fred Clarke, justified the creation of a post for a sociologist on the grounds that 'educational theory and educational policy that take no account of [sociological insights] will be not only blind but positively harmful' (quoted in Whitty, 1997: 4).[5]

Banks (1974: 21) has claimed that sociology 'has a particularly close and complicated relationship with social policy and political decision-making'. Although we sometimes tend to look back on the 1950s and 1960s as a 'golden age' in that relationship, Banks herself was sceptical about the extent to which even the political arithmetic tradition had influenced policymakers and indeed about the desirability of sociology doing so. However, Halsey (1972: 4) has argued that 'the task of the sociologist is, literally, to inform the political debate' and his own earlier work certainly did that. Arguably sociologists of education have been less involved in public policy debates recently, but their role in making sense of 'evidence' remains crucial, as I hope we have demonstrated in the discussion of widening participation policies in Chapter 5.

Sociology of education is not, of course, exempt from the more general problems in the contemporary relationship between educational research and education policy, which we discussed in Chapter 1. Furthermore, some of the concerns of sociologists are now taken for granted in the wider policy debate and do not therefore tend to be identified as specifically sociological insights. In addition, a number of sociologists have become identified with the more politically respectable tradition of school effectiveness and school improvement, although ironically one of the persistent criticisms of that work is its downplaying of the significance of social class (Hatcher, 1976; Coffield, 2011).

Some people would no doubt argue that, by focusing on work on education and social class here, I am understating the influence of the discipline on public policy. Particularly during the 1980s and 1990s, the sociology of education broadened its concerns to other social differences and social inequalities, notably gender, sexuality, 'race' and disability. And, especially in relation to gender, it could certainly claim some significant influence over policy. Now that the policy emphasis is again very much on social mobility and social class differences in education, although policymakers do not always use those terms, we need to make sure the voice of sociology is once again heard in that context, too. Even if not directly influencing policy or the political debate narrowly conceived, it should surely be contributing to wider public debate, even perhaps 'inoculating' the public mind against inappropriate policies as discussed in Chapter 3 of this book.

Thus, in my view, work in the sociology of education should currently be doing more to inform public debate and, where possible, encouraging the development of policies that help enhance levels of achievement and participation among working-class children. Although much of our work may suggest that most of the causes of the attainment gap are not within the remit of the school system, some of them undoubtedly are. For instance, in addition to the example given earlier concerning the curriculum, we can demonstrate that good teaching is especially important for disadvantaged pupils and that those students who do not have the sort of cultural capital that middle-class families provide at home need better access in school to information, advice and guidance on careers and university entrance (Curtis *et al.*, 2008).[6]

In some ways, then, the view that I reached about the importance of sociology of education in that Fabian Society Study Group at Cambridge 50 years ago remains my position today. That is why, in my valedictory interview at the Institute, I argued that the foundation disciplines, including the sociology of education, were 'mission critical' to an Institute of Education pursuing educational excellence for all and that they should therefore continue to have an important place in its portfolio of activities (Whitty, 2010b). But we have to recognize that, particularly in these days when research impact and public engagement are considered so important, the sociology of education will need to do a great deal more to justify that place in the public mind. I hope future generations of sociologists of education will make a better job of that than mine has.

Notes

[1] In terms of today's paradigm wars, it will be clear that I am closer to the social or critical realist camps than to the postmodernists and poststructuralists, although many of the writers I find most helpful defy easy categorization.

[2] I continued to take this view about the importance of quantitative research in the sociology of education even when it was unfashionable among the 'critical' sociologists of education with whose work my own was usually associated. See, for example, my interview with Carlos Torres in Torres (1998). It also influenced my determination as Director of the Institute of Education to encourage growth in quantitative research alongside the qualitative research that was already well established there.

[3] I hope the present chapter will indicate that my position is rather more sophisticated than that – as indeed I believe it was when I wrote that book 30 years ago. Christodoulou (2013) seems to have wilfully interpreted a casual comment about grammar school education as an epistemological claim, although I should certainly have made a clearer distinction in that comment between knowledge and pedagogy.

[4] Gove's allies accused Ofsted of favouring progressive teaching methods (see, for example, Christodoulou, 2013), something that Ofsted was forced to deny (Prynne, 2014).

[5] This was the post to which Mannheim was eventually appointed.

[6] This does not mean we should accept a deficit view of disadvantaged pupils but, even while subjecting the assumptions of higher education to critical scrutiny, we also need to facilitate entry to higher education as it is, as we argued in Chapter 5.

References

Adams, R. (2015) 'GCSE gap between rich and poor widens'. Online. www.theguardian.com/education/2015/jan/29/gcse-gap-rich-poor-widens (accessed 29 January 2015).

Alexander, C., Weekes-Bernard, D. and Arday, J. (eds) (2015) *The Runnymede School Report: Race, education and inequality in contemporary Britain*. London: Runnymede Trust.

Allen, G. (2011) *Early Intervention: The next steps: An independent report to Her Majesty's Government*. London: Cabinet Office.

Allen, R. (2010) 'Replicating Swedish free school reforms in England'. *Research in Public Policy*, 10, 4–7.

— (2012) 'How can London schools be so good, given the high cost of living for teachers?' IOE Blog, 22 May. Online. http://ioelondonblog.wordpress.com/2012/05/22/how-can-london-schools-be-so-good-given-the-high-cost-of-living-for-teachers/ (accessed 22 May 2012).

Allen, R., Belfield, C., Greaves, E., Sharp, C. and Walker, M. (2014) *The Costs and Benefits of Different Initial Teacher Training Routes*. London: Institute for Fiscal Studies.

Anders, J. (2012) 'The link between household income, university applications and university attendance'. *Fiscal Studies*, 33 (2), 185–210.

— (2015) *Private Pay Progression: Research brief 6 for upReach and The Sutton Trust*. London: The Sutton Trust.

Appadurai, A. (2004) 'The capacity to aspire: Culture and the terms of recognition'. In Rao, V. and Walton, M. (eds), *Culture and Public Action*. Stanford: Stanford University Press.

Apple, M. (1993) 'What post-modernists forget: Cultural capital and official knowledge'. *Curriculum Studies*, 1 (3), 301–16.

Archer, L. (2013) *ASPIRES: Young people's science and career aspirations, age 10–14*. London: Department of Education and Professional Studies, King's College London.

Archer, L., DeWitt, J., Osborne, J., Dillon, J., Willis, B. and Wong, B. (2012) 'Science aspirations, capital and family habitus: How families shape children's engagement and identification with science'. *American Educational Research Journal*, 49 (5), 881–909.

Archer, L., Hutchings, M. and Ross, A. (eds) (2002) *Higher Education and Social Class: Issues of exclusion and inclusion*. London: RoutledgeFalmer.

Archer, L. and Leathwood, C. (2003) 'Identities, inequalities and higher education'. In Archer, L., Hutchings, M. and Ross, A. (eds), *Higher Education and Social Class: Issues of exclusion and inclusion*. London: RoutledgeFalmer.

Arnett, G. (2015) 'Lies, damned lies and statistics: 220 potential MPs sign up for stats training'. *The Guardian*, 29 April. Online. www.theguardian.com/politics/datablog/2015/apr/29/potential-mps-general-election-2015-stats-training-numeracy (accessed 2 May 2015).

Arnett, T. (2015) *Startup Teacher Education: A fresh take on teacher credentialing*. San Mateo: Clayton Christensen Institute for Disruptive Innovation.

Association of School and College Leaders (ASCL) (2015) *Teacher Supply and Initial Teacher Education*. Leicester: Association of School and College Leaders.

Atherton, G., Cymbir, E., Roberts, K., Page, L. and Remedios, R. (2009) *How Young People Formulate their Views about the Future: Exploratory research*. DCSF Research Report 152. London: Department for Children, Schools and Families.

Auld, E. and Morris, P. (2014) 'Comparative education, the "New Paradigm" and policy borrowing: Constructing knowledge for educational reform'. *Comparative Education*, 50 (2), 129–55.

— (forthcoming) 'Marketing frames, leveraging expertise: Using PISA data to translate complex conditions into education "best practices"'. *Journal of Education Policy*.

Baars, S., Bernardes, E., Elwick, A., Malortie, A., McAleavy, T., McInerney, L., Menzies, L. and Riggall, A. (2014) *Lessons from London Schools: Investigating the success*. London: CfBT.

Baker, W., Sammons, P., Siraj-Blatchford, I., Sylva, K., Melhuish, E.C. and Taggart, B. (2014) 'Aspirations, education and inequality in England: Insights from the Effective Provision of Preschool, Primary and Secondary Education Project'. *Oxford Review of Education*, 40 (5), 525–42.

Ball, S. J. (1998) 'Big policies/small world: An introduction to international perspectives in education policy'. *Comparative Education*, 34 (2), 119–30.

— (2001) 'You've been NERFed! Dumbing down the academy. National Educational Research Forum "a national strategy—consultation paper": A brief and bilious response'. *Journal of Education Policy*, 16 (3), 265–8.

— (2003) *Class Strategies and the Education Market: The middle classes and social advantage*. London: Routledge.

— (2009) 'Privatising education, privatising education policy, privatising educational research: Network governance and the "competition state"'. *Journal of Education Policy*, 24 (1), 83–99.

— (2011a) 'Social class, families and the politics of educational advantage: The work of Denis Marsden'. *British Journal of Sociology of Education*, 32 (6), 957–65.

— (2011b) 'Attempting a theory of untidiness: An interview with Stephen J. Ball'. *Studia Paedagogica*, 16 (2), 159–69.

— (2012) *Global Education Inc.: New policy networks and the neo-liberal imaginary*. London: Routledge.

Ball, S. J. and Junemann, C. (2012) *Networks, New Governance and Education*. Bristol: Policy Press.

Ball, S. J., Maguire, M. and Macrae, S. (2000) *Choice, Pathways and Transitions Post-16: New youth, new economies in the global city*. London: Routledge.

Ball, S. J., Reay, D. and David, M. (2002) '"Ethnic choosing": Minority ethnic students and higher education choice'. *Race, Ethnicity and Education*, 5 (4), 333–57.

Bamfield, L. and Horton, T. (2010) *What's Fair? Applying the fairness test to education*. London: Fabian Society.

Banks, O. (1968) *The Sociology of Education*. London: Batsford.

— (1974) *Sociology and Education: An inaugural lecture*. Leicester: Leicester University Press.

Barber, M. (2005) 'Informed professionalism: Realising the potential'. Paper presented at the Association of Teachers and Lecturers conference, London, 11 June.

Barber, M., and Mourshed, M. (2007) *How the World's Best-Performing School Systems Come Out on Top*. London: McKinsey & Co.

Barrett, E., Barton. L., Furlong, J., Miles, E. and Whitty, G. (1992) *Initial Teacher Education in England and Wales: A topography*. London: Goldsmiths College.

Bassett, D., Haldenby, A., Tanner, W. and Threwhitt, K. (2010) 'Every teacher matters'. London: Reform. Online. www.reform.co.uk/wp-content/uploads/2014/10/Every-teacher-matters-FINAL1.pdf (accessed 15 April 2015).

Bastedo, M. and Gumport, P. (2003) 'Access to what? Mission differentiation and academic stratification in U.S. public higher education'. *Higher Education*, 46 (3), 341–59.

References

Bastow, S., Tinkler, J. and Dunleavy, P. (2014) *The Impact of the Social Sciences: How academics and their research make a difference*. London: Sage.

Bathmaker, A.-M., Ingram, N. and Waller, R. (2013) 'Higher education, social class and the mobilisation of capitals: Recognising and playing the game'. *British Journal of Sociology of Education*, 34 (5-06), 723–43.

Beck, J. (2012) 'Reinstating knowledge: Diagnostics and prescriptions for England's curriculum ills'. *International Studies in Sociology of Education*, 22 (1), 1–18.

Beck, M. (2015) 'Alternative teaching license measures to be redrawn in state budget'. Online. http://host.madison.com/news/local/govt-and-politics/alternative-teaching-license-measures-to-be-redrawn-in-state-budget/article_2e7cded8-7067-5bb6-8231-717cca7ed6a8.html (accessed 25 August 2015).

Bekhradnia, B. (2003) *Widening Participation and Fair Access: An overview of the evidence*. London: Higher Education Policy Institute.

Bell, D. (2012) 'Reflections on reform (Tribal Annual Education Lecture)'. London: Tribal. Online. www.tribalgroup.com/aboutus/events/Documents/Reflections%20on%20 Reform.pdf (accessed 24 November 2013).

Bennett, T. (2015) 'Evidence-based education is dead – long live evidence-informed education: Thoughts on Dylan Wiliam'. *Times Educational Supplement*, 11 April. Online. https://community.tes.co.uk/tom_bennett/b/weblog/archive/2015/04/11/evidence-based-education-is-dead-long-live-evidence-informed-education-thoughts-on-dylan-wiliam. aspx (accessed 18 April 2015).

BERA [British Educational Research Association] (2013) 'Why education research matters'. Online. www.bera.ac.uk/researchers-resources/publications/why-educational-research-matters-3 (accessed 5 April 2015).

— (2015) 'Research Intelligence'. Spring 2015. Online. www.bera.ac.uk/researchers-resources/publications/spring-2015 (accessed 10 April 2015).

BERA–RSA [British Educational Research Association – Royal Society for the encouragement of Arts, Manufactures and Commerce] (2014) *Research and the Teaching Profession: Building the capacity for a self-improving education system*. London: BERA. Online. www.bera.ac.uk/wp-content/uploads/2013/12/BERA-RSA-Research-Teaching-Profession-FULL-REPORT-for-web.pdf (accessed 19 May 2015).

BERA–UCET [British Educational Research Association – Universities' Council for the Education of Teachers] Working Group on Education Research (2012) *Prospects for Education Research in Education Departments in Higher Education Institutions in the UK*. London: British Educational Research Association. Online. www.bera.ac.uk/publications/bera-ucet-report (accessed 24 November 2013).

Beresford-Hill, P. (1993) 'Teacher education, access and quality control in higher education: Lessons from America for Britain's policy-makers'. *Oxford Review of Education* 19 (1), 79–88.

Bernstein, B. (1970) 'Education cannot compensate for society'. *New Society*, 15, 344–7.

— (1971) *Class, Codes and Control (Vol. 1)*. London: Routledge and Kegan Paul.

— (1977) *Class, Codes and Control (Vol. 3)*. London: Routledge and Kegan Paul.

— (1996) *Pedagogy, Symbolic Control and Identity*. London: Taylor and Francis.

Bhopal, K. and Preston, J. (eds) (2011) *Intersectionality and 'Race' in Education*. New York and London: Routledge.

BIS [Department for Business, Innovation and Skills] (2009a) *Skills for Growth: The national skills strategy*. London: The Stationery Office.

— (2009b) 'Full-time young participation by socio-economic class (FYPSEC): 2009 update'. London: BIS. Online. http://dera.ioe.ac.uk/9483/1/fypsec_paper_2009 (accessed 7 October 2015).

— (2009c) *Applications, Offers and Admissions to Research-Led Universities: A joint report by The Sutton Trust and the Department for Business, Innovation and Skills.* London: The Stationery Office.

— (2010) *The Role of Finance in the Decision-Making of Higher Education Applicants and Students, BIS Research Paper No. 9.* London: The Stationery Office.

— (2011) 'International comparative performance of the UK research base – 2011'. Online. www.gov.uk/government/uploads/system/uploads/attachment_data/file/32489/11-p123-international-comparative-performance-uk-research-base-2011.pdf (accessed 14 April 2015).

— (2014) *National Strategy for Access and Student Success.* London: BIS.

Black, P. and Wiliam, D. (1998) *Inside the Black Box: Raising standards through classroom assessment.* London: King's College London.

— (2003) '"In praise of educational research": Formative assessment'. *British Educational Research Journal*, 29 (5), 623–38.

Blair, T. (1996) Leader's speech presented to the Labour Party Conference, Blackpool, October. Online. www.britishpoliticalspeech.org/speech-archive.htm?speech=202 (accessed 10 April 2015).

Blanden, J., Greaves, E., Gregg, P., Macmillan, L. and Sibieta, L. (2015) 'Understanding the improved performance of disadvantaged pupils in London'. Social Policy in a Cold Climate Working Paper 21. London: Centre for the Analysis of Social Exclusion, London School of Economics and Political Science.

Blatchford, P. (2015) 'Moving on from the class size debate: A new project with a practical purpose'. Online. https://ioelondonblog.wordpress.com/2015/02/17/moving-on-from-the-class-size-debate-a-new-project-with-a-practical-purpose/ (accessed 12 May 2015).

Blatchford, P., Bassett, P., Brown, P., Martin, C. and Russell, A. (2004) *The Effects of Class Size on Attainment and Classroom Processes in English Primary Schools (Years 4 to 6) 2000–2003.* London: Department for Education and Skills.

Blatchford, P., Russell, A. and Webster, R. (2012) *Reassessing the Impact of Teaching Assistants: How research challenges practice and policy.* London: Routledge.

Blunkett, D. (2000) *Influence or Irrelevance: Can social science improve government?* London: Department for Education and Employment.

Bok, J. (2010) 'The capacity to aspire to higher education: "It's like making them do a play without a script"'. *Critical Studies in Education*, 51 (2), 163–78.

Boliver, V. (2008) 'Five decades of class inequality in British higher education'. Presentation delivered to University of Oxford Sociology Seminar, Oxford, 20 October.

— (2011) 'Expansion, differentiation, and the persistence of social class inequalities in British higher education'. *Higher Education* 61 (3), 229–42.

— (2013) 'How fair is access to more prestigious UK universities?', *British Journal of Sociology*, 64 (2), 344–64.

Bourdieu, P. (1986) 'The forms of capital'. In Richardson, J.G. (ed.) *Handbook of Theory and Research for the Sociology of Education.* New York: Greenwood Press.

Bourdieu, P. and Passeron, J-C. (1977) *Reproduction in Education, Society and Culture.* London: Sage.

Bourdieu, P. and Wacquant, L. (1992) *An Invitation to Reflexive Sociology.* Chicago: University of Chicago Press.

Bowles, S. and Gintis, H. (1976) *Schooling in Capitalist America.* London: Routledge and Kegan Paul.

References

Brighouse, T. (2007) 'The London Challenge – A personal view'. In Brighouse, T. and Fullick, L. (eds), *Education in a Global City: Essays from London*. London: Institute of Education.

Brown, C. (2014) *Making Evidence Matter: A new perspective for evidence-informed policy making in education*. London: IOE Press.

Brown, M. (2009) 'RAE 2008: Results, reflections and implications'. Online. www.bera.ac.uk/researchers-resources/publications/june-2009 (accessed 8 April 2015).

Burgess, S. (2014) *Understanding the Success of London's Schools*. Working Paper No. 14/333. Bristol: Centre for Market and Public Organisation.

Burke, P.J. (2012) *The Right to Higher Education*. Abingdon: Routledge.

Burke, P.J. and McManus, J. (2009) *Art for a Few: Exclusion and misrecognition in art and design higher education admissions*. London: National Arts Learning Network.

Calhoun, C. (2014) 'Paths to public influence: Social science in policy, debate and understanding'. Annual lecture presented to the Campaign for Social Science. London, 8 October. Online. https://campaignforsocialscience.org.uk/news/glass-half-full-social-science-campaign-annaul-lecture-hears/ (accessed 8 May 2015).

Callender, C. (2009) *Awareness, Take-up and Impact of Institutional Bursaries and Scholarships in England: Summary and recommendations*. Bristol: Office for Fair Access.

— (2010) 'Bursaries and institutional aid in higher education in England: Do they safeguard and promote fair access?' *Oxford Review of Education*, 36 (1), 45–62.

Callender, C. and Jackson, J. (2008) 'Does the fear of debt constrain choice of university and subject of study?' *Studies in Higher Education*, 33 (4), 405–29.

Callender, C. and Scott, P. (eds) (2013) *Browne and Beyond: Modernizing English higher education*. London: IOE Press.

Campaign for Social Science (2015) *The Business of People*. London: Sage. Online. http://campaignforsocialscience.org.uk/businessofpeople/ (accessed 18 May 2015).

Canada, G. (2010) Speech to the Conservative Party conference. Online. www.conservatives.com/Get_involved/Conference/Conference_2010.aspx (accessed 27 January 2011).

Carnegie Foundation (1992) *School Choice*. Princeton: Carnegie Foundation.

Carter, A. (2015) 'Carter review of initial teacher training'. London: DfE. Online. www.gov.uk/government/uploads/system/uploads/attachment_data/file/399957/Carter_Review.pdf (accessed 12 April 2015).

Cassen, R., McNally, S. and Vignoles, A. (2015) *Making a Difference in Education: What the evidence says*. Abingdon: Routledge.

Center for Education (2004) *Advancing Scientific Research in Education*. Washington: National Academies Press. Online. www.nap.edu/books/030909321X/html/ (accessed 6 April 2015).

Centre for Longitudinal Studies (2010) *Millenium Cohort Study Fourth Survey: A user's guide to initial findings*. London: Centre for Longitudinal Studies, Institute of Education.

Chowdry, H., Crawford, C., Dearden, L., Goodman, A. and Vignoles, A. (2010) *Widening Participation in Higher Education: Analysis using linked administrative data*. London: Institute for Fiscal Studies.

— (2013) 'Widening participation in higher education: Using linked administrative data'. *Journal of Royal Statistical Society (Series A)*, 176 (2), 431–57.

Christodoulou, D. (2013) *Seven Myths about Education*. London: The Curriculum Centre.

Chubb, J. and Moe, T. (1990) *Politics, Markets and America's Schools*. Washington, DC: Brookings Institution.

— (1992) *A Lesson in School Reform from Great Britain*. Washington, DC: Brookings Institution.

Claeys, A., Kempton, J. and Paterson, C. (2014) *Regional Challenges: A collaborative approach to improving education*. London: Centre Forum.

Clifton, J. and Cook, W. (2012) *A Long Division: Closing the attainment gap in England's secondary schools*. London: IPPR.

Coffield, F. (2011) 'Why the McKinsey reports will not improve school systems'. *Journal of Education Policy*, 27 (1), 1–19.

Coleman, J.S. (1988) 'Social capital in the creation of human capital'. *American Journal of Sociology*, 94(Suppl.), 95–120.

Collins, K. (2015) 'Dylan Wiliam is wrong to imply that teachers should shut the door to evidence'. *Times Educational Supplement*, 13 April. Online. www.tes.co.uk/news/school-news/breaking-views/dylan-wiliam-wrong-imply-teachers-should-shut-door-evidence (accessed 18 April 2015).

Cook, C. (2011) 'Poorer children close education gap'. *Financial Times*, 30 September. Online. www.ft.com/cms/s/0/d82fc3cc-eab3-11e0-aeca-00144feab49a.html (accessed 25 August 2015).

Corrigan, P. (1979) *Schooling the Smash Street Kids*. London: Macmillan.

Coyne, J. and Goodfellow, J.M. (2008) 'Report to the Secretary of State, DIUS, on universities' links with schools in STEM subjects'. Online. http://webarchive.nationalarchives.gov.uk/20100304105444/http://www.bis.gov.uk/policies/universities-links-in-stem-subjects (accessed 17 December 2015).

Craft, M. (1970) *Family, Class and Education: A reader*. London: Longman.

Crawford, C. (2012) *Socioeconomic Gaps in HE Participation: How have they changed over time?* London: Institute for Fiscal Studies.

— (2014) *The Link between Secondary School Characteristics and University Participation and Outcomes*. London: Department for Education.

Crozier, G., Reay, D., Clayton, J. and Colliander, L. (2008) *The Socio Cultural and Learning Experiences of Working Class Students in Higher Education*. Research Briefing 44. London: TLRP.

Cummings, C., Dyson, A., Muijs, D, Papps, I., Pearson, D., Raffo, C., Tiplady, L., Todd, L. and Crowther, D. (2007) *Evaluation of the Full Service Extended Schools Initiative: Final report*. DfES Research Report RR852. London: Department for Education and Skills.

Curtis, A. (2009) 'Academies and school diversity'. *Management in Education*, 23 (3), 113–17.

Curtis, A., Exley, S., Sasia, A., Tough, S. and Whitty, G. (2008) *The Academies Programme: Progress, problems and possibilities*. London: The Sutton Trust.

Curtis, A., Power, S., Whitty, G., Exley, S. and Sasia, A. (2008) *Primed for Success? The characteristics and practices of state schools with good track records of entry into prestigious UK universities*. London: The Sutton Trust.

David, M. (ed.) (2010) *Improving Learning by Widening Participation in Higher Education*. London: Routledge.

Davies, P. (2012) 'Can governments improve higher education through "informing choice"?'. *British Journal of Educational Studies*, 60 (3), 261–76.

Davies, P., Mangan, J. and Hughes, A. (2009) 'Participation, financial support and the marginal student'. *Higher Education*, 58 (2), 193–204.

Davies, P., Qiu, T. and Davies, N.M. (2014) 'Cultural and human capital, information and higher education choices'. *Journal of Education Policy*, 29 (6), 804–25.

Davies, P., Slack, K., Hughes, A., Mangan, J. and Vigurs, K. (2008) *Knowing Where to Study? Fees, bursaries and fair access*. London: The Sutton Trust.

References

Dawson, G. (1981) 'Unfitting teachers to teach: Sociology in the training of teachers'. In Flew, A., Marks, J., Cox, C., Honey, J., O'Keeffe, D., Dawson, G. and Anderson, D. (eds), *The Pied Pipers of Education*. London: Social Affairs Unit.

DCSF [Department for Children, Schools and Families] (2007) *The Children's Plan: Building brighter futures*. London: The Stationery Office.

— (2008) *Schools and Pupils in England: January 2007 (final). Statistical First Release 30/2007*. London: DCSF.

Dearden, L. and Jin, W. (2014) *The Rise and Demise of the National Scholarship Programme: Implications for university students*. London: Institute for Fiscal Studies.

Demack, S., Stevens, A. and McCaig, C. (2012) *'Dreams' and 'Realities' in University Access: Mapping social differences in higher education aspirations and participation in England*. London: Nuffield Foundation Report.

Department for Education [DfE] (2010a) *The Case for Change*. London: The Stationery Office.

— (2010b) *The Importance of Teaching*. London: The Stationery Office.

— (2011) *The National Strategies 1997–2011: A brief summary of the impact and effectiveness of the National Strategies. DfE Reference: 00032-2011*. London: Department for Education.

— (2014a) *Statistical First Release: GCSE and equivalent attainment by pupil characteristics in England, 2012/13*. London: Department for Education.

— (2014b) 'Experts to visit Shanghai to raise UK maths standards'. 18 February. London: Department for Education.

— (2015) 'New experts appointed to help improve initial teacher training'. 24 September. Online. www.gov.uk/government/news/new-experts-appointed-to-help-improve-initial-teacher-training (accessed 4 October 2015).

Department for Education and Skills [DfES] (2001) *Schools: Achieving success*. London: The Stationery Office. Online. www.gov.uk/government/uploads/system/uploads/attachment_data/file/355105/Schools_Achieving_Success.pdf (accessed 7 May 2015).

— (2003) *The Future of Higher Education*. London: The Stationery Office.

— (2005a) *Academies Evaluation–2nd Annual Report*. London: The Stationery Office.

— (2005b) *London Schools: Rising to the challenge*. London: Department for Education and Skills.

— (2006) 'Social mobility: Narrowing social class educational attainment gaps'. Supporting materials for a speech by the Rt. Hon. Ruth Kelly MP, Secretary of State for Education and Skills, to the Institute for Public Policy Research. London: Department for Education and Skills.

— (2007a) 'Secretary of State announces extension of the London Challenge programme'. Online. http://webarchive.nationalarchives.gov.uk/20070603200104/http://dfes.gov.uk/londonchallenge/news.shtml#announcement (accessed 25 August 2015).

— (2007b) *City Challenge for World Class Education*. London: Department of Education.

Department of Education and Science [DES] (1984) *Initial Teacher Training: Approval of courses (Circular 3/84)*. London: DES.

de Waal, A. (2008) *School Improvement – or the 'Equivalent'*. London: Civitas.

— (2009) *The Secrets of Academies' Success*. London: Civitas.

Diamond, I. (2005) 'Science and technology and international collaboration in higher education'. Lecture to the meeting of the UUK International and Longer-term Strategy Groups, March.

Doyle, M. and Griffin, M. (2012) 'Raised aspirations and attainment? A review of the impact of Aimhigher (2004–2011) on widening participation in higher education in England'. *London Review of Education*, 10 (1), 75–88.

Earl, L., Levin, B., Leithwood, K., Fullan, M. and Watson, N. (2001) *OISE/UT Evaluation of the Implementation of the National Literacy and Numeracy Strategies. Second annual report: Watching & Learning 2. DfES Report DfES-0617/2001.* London: Department for Education and Skills.

Earley, P. and Weindling, D. (2006) 'Consultant leadership: A new role for head teachers?' *School Leadership & Management*, 26 (1), 37–53.

Edwards, A.D. (1976) *Language in Culture and Class: The sociology of language and education.* London: Heinemann.

Edwards, A.D., Fitz, J. and Whitty, G. (1989) *The State and Private Education: An evaluation of the assisted places scheme.* London: Falmer Press.

EEF [Education Endowment Foundation] (2012) 'Teaching and learning toolkit'. Online. http://educationendowmentfoundation.org.uk/toolkit/ (accessed 10 December 2013).

Elliott, R. (ed.) (2008) *Brands and Brand Management.* London: Routledge.

Evans, R. (2011) 'Is the Canadian model right for UK schools?' *The Guardian*, 4 January. Online. www.theguardian.com/education/2011/jan/04/education-policy-canadian-model (accessed 25 August 2015).

Exley, S. and Ball, S.J. (2011) 'Something old, something new ... understanding Conservative education policy'. In Bochel, H. (ed.), *The Conservative Party and Social Policy.* Bristol: Policy Press.

Eyles, A. and Machin, S. (2015) *The Introduction of Academy Schools to England's Education. CEP Discussion Paper No. 1368.* London: Centre for Economic Performance, LSE.

Fantini, M. and Weinstein, G. (1968) *The Disadvantaged: Challenge to education.* New York: Harper and Row.

Field, F. (2010) *The Foundation Years: Preventing poor children becoming poor adults. The report of the Independent Review on Poverty and Life Chances.* London: Cabinet Office.

Finegold, D., McFarland, L. and Richardson, W. (eds) (1993) *Something Borrowed, Something Learned? The transatlantic market in education and training reform.* Washington, DC: Brookings Institution.

Fischetti, J. (2014). 'Issues in education: The rubber duckies are here: Five trends affecting publication around the world'. *Childhood Education*, 90 (4), 316–18.

Floud, J. (1959) 'Karl Mannheim'. In Judges, A.V. (ed.), *The Function of Teaching.* London: Faber and Faber.

Floud, J., Halsey, A.H. and Martin, F. (1956) *Social Class and Educational Opportunity.* London: Heinemann.

Furlong, J. (2005) 'New Labour and teacher education: The end of an era'. *Oxford Review of Education*, 31 (1), 119–34.

— (2008) 'Making teaching a 21st century profession: Tony Blair's big prize'. *Oxford Review of Education*, 34 (6), 727–39.

— (2013) *Education: An anatomy of the discipline.* London: Routledge.

Furlong, J., Barton, L., Miles, S., Whiting, C. and Whitty, G. (2000) *Teacher Education in Transition: Re-forming professionalism?* Buckingham: Open University Press.

Gale, T. (2015) 'Widening and expanding participation in Australian higher education: In the absence of sociological imagination'. *The Australian Educational Researcher*, 42 (2), 257–71.

Gale, T. and Densmore, K. (2003) *Engaging Teachers: Towards a radical democratic agenda for schooling.* Maidenhead: Open University Press.

Gale, T. and Hodge, S. (2014) 'Just imaginary: Delimiting social inclusion in higher education'. *British Journal of Sociology of Education*, 35 (5), 688–709.

References

Gamarnikow, E. and Green, A. (1999) 'Developing social capital: Dilemmas, possibilities and limitations in education'. In Hayton, A. (ed.), *Tackling Disaffection and Social Exclusion: Education perspectives and policies*. London: Kogan Page.

Gamble, A. (1994) *The Free Economy and the Strong State: The politics of Thatcherism*, 2nd edition. Basingstoke: Palgrave Macmillan.

Gardiner, J. (1997) 'Marriage of maximum inconvenience?' *Times Educational Supplement*, 6 June.

Garner, R. (2009) 'Poor students "priced out of university by top-up fees"'. *The Independent*, 5 June, 17. Online. www.independent.co.uk/news/education/education-news/poor-students-priced-out-of-university-by-topup-fees-1697318.html (accessed 25 August 2015).

— (2015) 'Panic rush for university places predicted'. *The Independent*, 10 August. Online. www.pressreader.com/uk/the-independent/20150810/281487865073172/TextView (accessed 1 October 2015).

Gerrard, J. (2015) 'Public education in neoliberal times: Memory and desire'. *Journal of Education Policy*, 30 (6), 855–68.

Gewirtz, S. (2001) 'Cloning the Blairs: New Labour's programme for the re-socialization of working-class parents'. *Journal of Educational Policy*, 16 (4), 365–78.

— (2003) 'Enlightening the research–policy relationship: Issues and dilemmas for educational researchers'. Paper presented at the European Conference on Educational Research, University of Hamburg, Germany, 17–20 September.

Gillborn, D. (2014) 'Changing benchmarks restore black/white inequality'. Presentation to the Centre for Research in Race and Education, University of Birmingham.

— (2015) 'Intersectionality, critical race theory, and the primacy of racism: Race, class, gender, and disability in education'. *Qualitative Inquiry*, 21 (3), 277–87.

Gillborn, D. and Mirza, H. (2000) *Educational Inequality: Mapping race, class and gender*. London: Ofsted.

Glass, G.V. (1987) 'What works: Politics and research'. *Educational Researcher*, 16 (3), 5–10.

Goldacre, B. (2013) *Building Evidence into Education*. London: Department for Education. www.gov.uk/government/news/building-evidence-into-education (accessed 30 April 2015).

Goldstein, H. (2001) 'The 2001 Education White Paper and evidence based policy: A commentary'. London: Institute of Education. Online. www.bristol.ac.uk/media-library/sites/cmm/migrated/documents/educationwhitepaper2001.pdf (accessed 17 December 2015).

— (2002) *The National Literacy and Numeracy Strategy (NLNS) Evaluation: Part 2*. Bristol: Centre for Multilevel Modelling, University of Bristol. Online. www.bristol.ac.uk/cmm/team/hg/oisereport2.html (accessed 25 August 2015).

Gorard, S. (2005) 'Academies as the "future of schooling": Is this an evidence-based policy?' *Journal of Education Policy*, 20 (3), 369–77.

Gorard, S. and See, B.H. (2013) *Overcoming Disadvantage in Education*. London: Routledge.

Gorard, S., See, B.H. and Davies, P. (2012) *The Impact of Attitudes and Aspirations on Educational Attainment and Participation*. York: Joseph Rowntree Foundation.

Gore, J. and Bowe, J. (2015) 'Interrupting attrition? Re-shaping the transition from preservice to inservice teaching through quality teaching rounds'. *International Journal of Education Research* (in press). doi:10.1016/j.ijer.2015.05.006 (accessed 25 August 2015).

Gough, D., Oliver, S. and Thomas, J. (eds) (2012) *An Introduction to Systematic Reviews*. London: Sage.

Gould, J. (1977) *The Attack on Higher Education: Marxist and radical penetration*. London: Institute for the Study of Conflict.

Gove, M. (2008) 'Higher standards, freer minds'. Presented at Haberdashers' Aske's Education Lecture, Haberdashers Hall, London, 18 November.
— (2010) 'Michael Gove to Westminster Academy'. Speech to Westminster Academy, 6 September. Online. www.education.gov.uk/inthenews/speeches/a0064281/michael-gove-to-westminster-academy (accessed 15 November 2010).
— (2011) 'A liberal education'. Speech to Cambridge University, 24 November 2011.
— (2012) 'Michael Gove at the National College annual conference'. 14 June. Online. www.gov.uk/government/speeches/michael-gove-at-the-national-college-annual-conference (accessed 12 July 2012).
— (2013a) 'I refuse to surrender to the Marxist teachers hell-bent on destroying our schools: Education Secretary berates "the new enemies of promise" for opposing his plans'. *Daily Mail*, 23 March. Online. http://goo.gl/5SQBe (accessed 24 November 2013).
— (2013b) 'Michael Gove speaks about the importance of teaching'. Speech to the Policy Exchange, London, 5 September. Online. www.gov.uk/government/speeches/michael-gove-speaks-about-the-importance-of-teaching (accessed 24 November 2013).
Greaves, E., Macmillan, L. and Sibieta, L. (2014) *Lessons from London Schools for Attainment Gaps and Social Mobility*. London: Institute for Fiscal Studies.
Green, D. (1991) 'Lessons from America'. In Green, D. (ed.), *Empowering the Parents: How to break the schools' monopoly*. London: Institute of Economic Affairs.
Grek, S. (2008) *PISA in the British media: Leaning tower or robust testing tool? CES Briefing No. 45, April 2008*. Online. www.ces.ed.ac.uk/PDF%20Files/Brief045.pdf (accessed 15 November 2010).
Griffiths, S. (2010) 'Me and my 350 schools'. *The Times*, 21 February. Online. www.timesonline.co.uk/tol/life_and_style/education/article7034772.ece (accessed 15 November 2010).
Gulson, K. and Metcalfe, A. (2015) 'Introduction: Education policy analysis for a complex world: Poststructural possibilities'. *Critical Studies in Education*, 56 (1), 1–4.
Haddon, C., Devanny, J., Forsdick, C. and Thompson, A. (2015) 'What is the value of history in policymaking?' Online. www.instituteforgovernment.org.uk/sites/default/files/publications/Making%20History%20Work%20Report%20-%20Final_0.pdf (accessed 10 May 2015).
Halsey, A.H. (1972) *Educational Priority. Vol 1*. London: HMSO.
Halsey, A.H., Floud, J.E. and Anderson, C.A. (eds) (1961) *Education, Economy, and Society*. New York: Free Press.
Halsey, A.H., Heath, A. and Ridge, J. (1980) *Origins and Destinations*. Oxford: Clarendon Press.
Hargreaves, A. (2008) 'Engaging policy: Neither a borrower nor a lender be'. In Chakroun, B. and Sahlberg, P. (eds), *European Training Foundation Yearbook*. Luxembourg: European Training Foundation.
Hargreaves, D. (1967) *Social Relations in a Secondary School*. London: Routledge and Kegan Paul.
— (1996) *Teaching as a Research-Based Profession*. London: Teacher Training Agency.
Harris, M. (2010) *What More Can Be Done to Widen Access to Highly Selective Universities? A report from Sir Martin Harris, Director of Fair Access*. Bristol: OFFA.
Harrison, N., James, D. and Last, K. (2015) 'Don't know what you've got 'til it's gone? Skills-led qualifications, secondary school attainment and policy choices'. *Research Papers in Education*, 30 (5), 585–608.

References

Harrison, N. and Waller, R. (2010) 'We blame the parents! A response to "Cultural capital as an explanation of variation in participation in higher education" by John Noble and Peter Davies'. *British Journal of Sociology of Education*, 31 (4), 471–82.

Hatcher, R. (1976) 'The limitations of the new social democratic agenda'. In Hatcher, R. and Jones, K. (eds) *Education after the Conservatives*. Stoke-on-Trent: Trentham Books.

Hattie, J. (2008) *Visible Learning: A synthesis of over 800 meta-analyses relating to achievement*. Abingdon: Routledge.

HEFCE [Higher Education Funding Council for England] (2011a) 'Assessment framework and guidance on submissions'. www.ref.ac.uk/pubs/2011-02/ (accessed 10 April 2015).

— (2011b) 'National Scholarship Programme 2012–13: Guidance for institutions'. Circular letter 10/2011. Bristol: HEFCE.

— (2014a) 'Guidance for national networks for collaborative outreach'. Circular letter 20/2014. Bristol: HEFCE.

— (2014b) 'Creating and sustaining the conditions for a world-leading higher education system'. *HEFCE Draft Business Plan, 2015–2020*. Bristol: HEFCE.

— (2015) 'Delivering opportunities for students and maximising their success: Evidence for policy and practice 2015–2020'. Bristol: HEFCE.

Henig, J.R. (2008) *Spin Cycle: How research is used in policy debates – The case of charter schools*. New York: Russell Sage Foundation.

Her Majesty's Inspectorate of Schools [HMI] (1989) *The Provisional Teacher Program in New Jersey*. London: HMSO.

— (1990) *Teaching and Learning in New York City Schools*. London: HMSO.

Higher Education Statistics Agency [HESA] (2009) *PIs 2007/08: Widening participation of under-represented groups (Tables T1, T2)*. Cheltenham: HESA.

Hill, D., McLaren, P., Cole, M. and Rikowski, G. (2002) *Marxism against Postmodernism in Educational Theory*. Lanham: Lexington Books.

Hillage, J., Pearson, R., Anderson, A. and Tamkin, P. (1998) *Excellence in Research in Schools*. London: Department for Education and Employment.

Hillgate Group (1987) *The Reform of British Education: From principles to practice*. London: Claridge Press.

Hillman, N. (2014) *A Guide to the Removal of Student Number Controls*. Oxford: Higher Education Policy Institute.

Hills, J., Brewer, M., Jenkins, S., Lister, R., Lupton, R., Machin, S., Mills, C., Modood, T., Rees, T. and Riddell, S. (2010) *An Anatomy of Economic Inequality in the UK: Report of the National Equality Panel, CASE report 60*. London: Centre for Analysis of Social Exclusion, London School of Economics and Political Science.

Hirsch, E.D. (1999) *The Schools We Need: And why we don't have them*, 2nd edition. New York: Anchor Books.

Hirst, P.H. (1969) 'The Logic of the curriculum'. *Journal of Curriculum Studies*, 1, 142–58.

Her Majesty's Government [HM Government] (2010a) *The Coalition: Our programme for government*. London: Cabinet Office.

— (2010b) *Opening Doors, Breaking Barriers: A strategy for social mobility*. London: Cabinet Office. Online. www.gov.uk/government/publications/opening-doors-breaking-barriers-a-strategy-for-social-mobility (accessed 1 October 2015).

Her Majesty's Chief Inspectorate [HMCI] (2011) *Annual Report of Her Majesty's Chief Inspector of Education, Children's Services and Skills 2010–11*. London: Ofsted.

House of Commons [HoC] (2010) *Training of Teachers: Fourth report of the House of Commons Children, Schools and Families Committee 2009–10*. London: The Stationery Office.

— (2012) *Great Teachers: Attracting, training and retaining the best. Ninth Report of the House of Commons Education Committee 2010–12.* London: The Stationery Office.

— (2015) *Academies and Free Schools. Fourth Report of the Education Committee for the Session 2014–15.* London: The Stationery Office.

House of Commons Education and Skills Select Committee (2005) *Secondary Education. Fifth report of session 2004–05.* London: The Stationery Office. Online. www.publications.parliament.uk/pa/cm200405/cmselect/cmeduski/86/86.pdf (accessed 12 April 2015).

House of Commons Education Select Committee (2011) 'Uncorrected transcript of oral evidence: Oral evidence taken before the education committee: Attracting, training and retaining the best teachers'. Online. www.publications.parliament.uk/pa/cm201012/cmselect/cmeduc/uc1515-iii/uc151501.htm (accessed 4 October 2015).

— (2013) *Careers Guidance for Young People: The impact of the new duty on schools: Seventh report of session 2012–13, HC 632-i.* London: The Stationery Office.

— (2015) *Academies and Free Schools. Fourth Report of the Education Committee for the Session 2014-15.* London: The Stationery Office. Online. www.publications.parliament.uk/pa/cm201415/cmselect/cmeduc/258/258.pdf (accessed 12 April 2015).

House of Commons Public Administration Select Committee (2009) *Good Government, Eighth Report of the Session 2008–09, Vol. II: Oral and written evidence. HC 97-II.* London: The Stationery Office.

House of Commons Science and Technology Committee (2009) *Evidence Check 1: Early literacy interventions.* London: The Stationery Office. Online. www.publications.parliament.uk/pa/cm200910/cmselect/cmsctech/44/4407.htm (accessed 31 October 2015).

Hodgkinson, P. (2000) 'Who wants to be a social engineer? A commentary on David Blunkett's speech to the ESRC'. *Sociological Research Online*, 5 (1). Online. http://socresonline.org.uk/5/1/hodgkinson.html (accessed 10 April 2015).

Holmwood, J. (2015) 'Social scientists shouldn't shy away from political debates'. *The Guardian*, 12 March. Online. www.theguardian.com/higher-education-network/2015/mar/12/social-scientists-shouldnt-shy-away-from-political-debates (accessed 18 June 2015).

Hurst, G. (2013) 'Get out of the ivory towers, academics told'. *The Times*, 21 March. Online. www.thetimes.co.uk/tto/education/article3718769.ece (accessed 29 November 2013).

Hutchings, M., Greenwood, C., Hollingworth, S., Mansaray, A., Rose, A., Minty, S. and Glass, K. (2012) 'Evaluation of the City Challenge programme'. *DfE Research Report DFE-RR215.* London: Institute for Policy Studies in Education, London Metropolitan University.

Hutchings, M., Francis, B. and de Vries, R. (2014) *Chain Effects: The impact of academy chains on low income students.* London: The Sutton Trust.

Hutchings, M., Francis, B. and Kirby, P. (2015) *Chain Effects 2015: The impact of academy chains on low income students.* London: The Sutton Trust.

Jackson, B. and Marsden, D. (1962) *Education and the Working Class.* Harmondsworth: Penguin.

Jadad, A.R. and Enkin, M.W. (2007) *Randomized Controlled Trials: Questions, answers and musings.* London: Wiley.

Iannelli, C. (2013) 'The role of the school curriculum in social mobility'. *British Journal of Sociology of Education*, 34 (6), 907–28.

Independent Commission on Fees [ICOF] (2014) *Analysis of Trends in Higher Education Applications, Admissions, and Enrolments, August 2014.* London: Independent Commission on Fees.

Jerrim, J. (2012) 'The socio-economic gradient in teenagers' reading skills: How does England compare with other countries?' *Fiscal Studies*, 53 (2), 159–84.

Jerrim, J. and Vignoles, A. (2015) 'The causal effect of East Asian 'mastery' teaching methods on English children's mathematics skills'. Online. https://johnjerrim.files.wordpress.com/2013/07/mm_paper_june_2015.pdf (accessed 25 August 2015).

References

Johnes, G. and McNabb, R. (2004) 'Never give up on the good times: Student attrition in the UK'. *Oxford Bulletin of Economics and Statistics*, 66, 23–47.

Jump, P. (2015) 'REF 2014 impact case studies: Government policy cited most'. *Times Higher Education*, 26 March. Online. www.timeshighereducation.co.uk/news/ref-2014-impact-case-studies-government-policy-cited-most/2019291.article (accessed 9 April 2015).

Keay, D. (1987) 'An interview with Margaret Thatcher'. *Woman's Own*, 31 October.

Keddie, N. (1973) *Tinker, Tailor... The Myth of Compensatory Education*. Harmondsworth: Penguin.

Kelly, K. and Cook, S. (2007) 'Full-time young participation by socio-economic class: A new widening participation measure in higher education'. *DfES Research Report RR806*. Online. http://dera.ioe.ac.uk/6555/1/RR806.pdf (accessed 1 October 2015).

Kelly, R. (2005a) 'Education and social progress'. Keynote speech to the Institute for Public Policy Research, July.

— (2005b) Speech to North of England Education Conference, Manchester, 6 January.

Kerr, K. and West, M. (eds) (2010) *Social Inequality: Can schools narrow the gap? Insight 2*. Chester: British Educational Research Association.

Lacey, C. (1970) *Hightown Grammar*. Manchester: Manchester University Press.

Laurison, D. and Friedman, S. (2015) 'Introducing the class ceiling: Social mobility into Britain's elite occupations'. LSE Sociology Department Working Paper. London: London School of Economics and Political Science.

Lawlor, S. (1990) *Teachers Mistaught: Training in theories or education in subjects?* London: Centre for Policy Studies.

Lawton, D. (2005) *Education and Labour Party Ideologies: 1900–2001 and beyond*. London: RoutledgeFalmer.

Leathwood, C. and Hayton, A. (2002) 'Educational inequalities in the UK: A critical analysis of the discourses and policies of New Labour'. *Australian Journal of Education*, 46 (2), 138–53.

Levin, B. (1998) 'An epidemic of education policy: (What) can we learn from each other?' *Comparative Education*, 34 (2), 131–41.

Linehan, P. (ed.) (2011) *St John's College, Cambridge: A history*. Woodbridge: Boydell Press.

Lucas, S. (2001) 'Effectively maintained inequality: Education transitions, track mobility, and social background effects'. *American Journal of Sociology*, 106 (6), 1,642–90.

Lupton, R. and Obolenskaya, P. (2013) 'Labour's record on education: Policy, spending and outcomes 1997–2010'. Social Policy in A Cold Climate Working Papers. London: Centre for Analysis of Social Exclusion, London School of Economics.

MacDonald, B. (1974) 'Evaluation and the control of education'. Reprinted in Murphy, R. and Torrance, H. (eds) (1987) *Evaluating Education: Issues and methods*. London: Harper and Row.

Machin, S. and McNally, S. (2004) 'The literacy hour'. CEE Discussion Paper 43. London: Centre for the Economics of Education, London School of Economics.

Machin, S., McNally, S. and Meghir, C. (2007) *Resources and Standards in Urban Schools*. London: Centre for the Economics of Education.

Machin, S. and Silva, O. (2013) 'School structure, school autonomy and the tail'. Special Paper 29. London: Centre for Economic Performance, London School of Economics. Online. http://cep.lse.ac.uk/pubs/download/special/cepsp29.pdf (accessed 25 August 2015).

Machin, S. and Vernoit, J. (2011) 'Changing school autonomy: Academy schools and their introduction to England's education'. CEE Discussion Paper 123. London: Centre for the Economics of Education, London School of Economics. Online. http://cee.lse.ac.uk/ceedps/ceedp123.pdf (accessed 25 August 2015).

MacLure, M. (2005) '"Clarity bordering on stupidity": Where's the quality in systematic review?' *Journal of Education Policy*, 20 (4), 393–416.

Maddern, K. (2013) 'Teacher training turmoil sparks fears of recruitment crisis'. *Times Educational Supplement*, 12 April.

Maden, M. (ed.) (2002) *Success against the Odds Five Years On*. London: Routledge.

McAleavy, T. and Elwick, A. (2015) *School Improvement in London: A global perspective*. London: CfBT.

Mangan, J., Hughes, A., Davies, P. and Slack, K. (2010) 'Fair access: Explaining the association between social class and students' choice of university'. *Studies in Higher Education*, 35 (3), 335–50.

Mann, H. (1844) *Mr. Mann's Seventh Annual Report: Education in Europe*. Boston, MA: Massachusetts Board of Education.

Mannheim, K. and Stewart, W.A.C. (1962) *An Introduction to the Sociology of Education*. London: Routledge and Kegan Paul.

Mansell, W. (2005) 'Why this man scares Ruth Kelly'. *Times Educational Supplement*, 26 August.

— (2014) 'Parents say rejection of Institute of Education free school plan is "political"'. *The Guardian*, 25 February. Online. www.theguardian.com/education/2014/feb/25/institute-education-free-school-plans-turned-down (accessed 25 August 2015).

Manville, C., Jones, M.M., Frearson, M., Castle-Clark, S., Henham, M., Gunashekar, S. and Grant, J. (2015) *Preparing Impact Submissions for REF 2014: An evaluation. Findings and observations*. Online. www.hefce.ac.uk/pubs/rereports/Year/2015/REFimpacteval/Title,103726,en.html (accessed 12 April 2015).

Mathis, W. (2012) *Research-based Options for Education Policymaking: Teacher evaluation*. Boulder, CO: National Education Policy Center.

Mathis, W. and Welner, K. (2010) *The Obama Education Blueprint: Researchers examine the evidence*. Boulder, CO: National Education Policy Center.

McCaig, C. (2016) 'The retreat from widening participation? The National Scholarship Programme and new access agreements in English higher education'. *Studies in Higher Education*, 41 (2), 215–30.

McCrone, T., Marshall, H., White, K., Reed, F., Morris, M., Andrews, D. and Barnes, A. (2009) 'Careers coordinators in schools'. Research Report 171. London: Department of Children, Families and Schools.

McKnight, A. (2015) 'Downward mobility, opportunity hoarding and the "glass floor"'. Research Report by Centre for Analysis of Social Exclusion (CASE), London School of Economics. London: Social Mobility and Child Poverty Commission.

McNally, S. (2015) *Schools: The evidence on academies, resources and pupil performance*. London: Centre for Economic Performance, London School of Economics.

Menzies, L. (2013) *Educational Aspirations: How English schools can work with parents to keep them on track*. York: Joseph Rowntree Foundation.

Michie, J. and Cooper, C. (eds) (2015) *Why the Social Sciences Matter*. Basingstoke: Palgrave Macmillan.

Milburn, A. (2009) *Unleashing Aspiration: The final report of the Panel on Fair Access to the Professions*. London: Cabinet Office.

Miliband, D. (1991) *Markets, Politics and Education: Beyond the Education Reform Act*. London: Institute for Public Policy Research.

Miliband, E. (2014) Speech to the Labour Party Annual Conference, Manchester. Online. http://press.labour.org.uk/post/98234398144/speech-by-ed-miliband-to-laboursannualconference (accessed 5 November 2014).

Moore, C. (2013) 'The Spectator's Notes'. *The Spectator*, 9 November.

References

Morris, P. (2015) 'Comparative education, PISA, politics and educational reform: A cautionary note'. *Compare*, 45 (3), 470–4.

Morris, R. (2015) 'Free schools and disadvantaged intakes'. *British Educational Research Journal*, 41 (4), 535–52.

Mortimore, P. and Whitty, G. (1997) *Can School Improvement Overcome the Effects of Disadvantage?* London: Institute of Education.

Muijs, D., Chapman, C. and Armstrong, P. (2010) *Maximum Impact Evaluation: The impact of Teach First teachers in schools*. Final Report. Manchester: University of Manchester.

Mulgan, G. and Puttick, R. (2013) *Making Evidence Useful: The case for new institutions*. London: NESTA. Online. www.nesta.org.uk/sites/default/files/making_evidence_useful.pdf (accessed 18 May 2015).

NAO [National Audit Office] (2007) *The Academies Programme. Report by the Comptroller and Auditor General HC 254 Session 2005–2007*. London: The Stationery Office.

NatCen [National Centre for Social Research] (2011) 'Evaluation of "Every Child a Reader"'. DfE Research Report DFE-RR114. London: Department for Education.

Nathan, J. (1996) *Charter Schools: Creating hope and opportunity for American education*. San Francisco: Jossey-Bass.

National Board for Educational Sciences (2010) 'Director's final proposed priorities for the Institute of Education Sciences'. Online. http://ies.ed.gov/director/board/priorities.asp (accessed 31 January 2010).

National Commission on Education (1993) *Learning to Succeed: A radical look at education today and a strategy for the future*. London: Heinemann.

NERF [National Educational Research Forum] (2000) 'A national strategy'. Consultation paper issued by the National Educational Research Forum. London: NERF.

— (2001) *A Research and Development Strategy for Education: Developing quality and diversity*. London: NERF.

Nelson, J. and O'Beirne, C. (2014) 'Using evidence in the classroom: What works and why? Research summary'. Slough: NfER. Online. www.nfer.ac.uk/publications/IMPA01/IMPA01.pdf (accessed 17 May 2015).

NESS [National Evaluation of Sure Start Team] (2010) 'The Impact of Sure Start Local Programmes on five year olds and their families'. DfE Research Report DFE-RR067. London: Department for Education.

Nisbet, J. (1974) 'Educational Research: The state of the art'. Address to the Inaugural Meeting of the British Educational Research Association, Birmingham, April.

Noble, J. and Davies, P. (2009) 'Cultural capital as an explanation of variation in participation in higher education'. *British Journal of Sociology of Education*, 30 (5), 591–605.

Nutley, S.M., Walter, I. and Davies, H.T.O. (2007) *Using Evidence: How research can inform public services*. Bristol: The Policy Press.

Nutley, S., Powell, A. and Davies, H. (2013) 'What counts as good evidence? Provocation paper for the Alliance for Useful Evidence'. London: Alliance for Useful Evidence. Online. www.alliance4usefulevidence.org/assets/What-Counts-as-Good-Evidence-WEB.pdf (accessed 18 May 2015).

O'Hear, A. (1988) *Who Teaches the Teachers?* London: Social Affairs Unit.

Oakley, A. (2000) *Experiments in Knowing: Gender and method in the social sciences*. Cambridge: Polity Press.

— (2002) 'Social science and evidence-based everything: The case of education'. *Educational Review*, 54 (3), 277–86.

Obama, B. (2010) 'A letter from the President'. In United States Department of Education, *A Blueprint for Reform: The Reauthorization of the Elementary and Secondary Education Act.* Washington, DC: United States Department of Education. Online. www2.ed.gov/policy/elsec/leg/blueprint/blueprint.pdf (accessed 15 November 2010).

OECD [Organisation for Economic Co-operation and Development] (2010) *Strong Performance and Successful Reformers in Education: Lessons from PISA for the United States.* Paris: OECD Publishing. Online. www.oecd.org/pisa/46623978.pdf (accessed 4 October 2015).

OECD (2015) *Education Policy Outlook 2015: Making reforms happen.* Paris: OECD Publishing. Online. http://dx.doi.org/10.1787/9789264225442-en (accessed 20 October 2015).

OFFA [Office for Fair Access] (2004) *Producing Access Agreements – Guidance November 2004/01.* Bristol: Office of Fair Access.

— (2014) *Trends in Young Participation by Student Background and Selectivity of Institution.* Bristol: OFFA.

Office for Standards in Education, Children's Services and Skills [Ofsted] (2010a) *London Challenge. Report number 100192.* London: Ofsted.

— (2010b) *The National Strategies: A review of impact. Report number 080272.* London: Ofsted.

— (2012) *The Pupil Premium: How schools are using the Pupil Premium funding to raise achievement for disadvantaged pupils.* London: Ofsted.

— (2013a) 'School-led partnerships setting the benchmark for high quality teacher training'. Press release, 22 March (amended). London: Ofsted. Online. www.ofsted.gov.uk/news/school-led-partnerships-setting-benchmark-for-high-quality-teacher-training-0 (accessed 29 November 2013).

— (2013b) 'Going in the right direction? Careers guidance in schools from 2012'. Report No. 130114. Manchester: Office for Standards in Education, Children's Services and Skills.

— (2013c) *Unseen Children: Access and achievement 20 years on.* London: Ofsted.

— (2014a) *The Pupil Premium: An update.* London: Ofsted.

— (2014b) *Ofsted Annual Report 2013/14.* London: Ofsted.

ONS [Office for National Statistics] (2006) *Statistics of Education: Trends in attainment gaps: 2005.* London: Office for National Statistics.

Ovenden-Hope, T. and Passy, R. (2013) *Coastal Academies: Meeting the challenge of school improvement.* Plymouth: Plymouth University.

Paton, G. (2012) 'University access tsar: Institutions "must set tougher admissions targets"'. *The Daily Telegraph*, 6 September. Online. www.telegraph.co.uk/education/universityeducation/9522485/University-access-tsar-institutions-must-set-tougher-admissions-targets.html (accessed 25 August 2015).

Phillips, D. and Ochs, K. (2003) 'Processes of policy borrowing in education: Some explanatory and analytical devices'. *Comparative Education*, 39 (4), 451–61.

Pollard, A. (2015) 'Achievement, divergence and opportunity in education: Some outcomes and challenges of REF 2014'. *Research Intelligence*, 126, 10–11. Online. www.bera.ac.uk/wp-content/uploads/2015/03/RI-Issue-127.pdf (accessed 10 April 2015).

Porter, N. and Simons, J. (2015) *A Rising Tide: The competitive benefits of free schools.* London: Policy Exchange.

Power, S., Brannen, J., Brown, A. and Chisholm, L. (2001) *A Tribute to Basil Bernstein, 1924–2000.* London: Institute of Education.

Power, S, Edwards, T., Whitty, G. and Wigfall, V. (2003) *Education and the Middle Class.* Buckingham: Open University Press.

Power, S. and Whitty, G. (2006) 'Education and the middle class: A complex but crucial case for the sociology of education'. In Lauder, H., Brown, P., Dillabough, J. and Halsey, A.H. (eds), *Education, Globalization and Social Change.* Oxford: Oxford University Press.

References

Power, S., Whitty, G., Gewirtz, S., Halpin, D. and Dickson, M. (2004) 'Paving a "Third way"? A policy trajectory analysis of Education Action Zones'. *Research Papers in Education*, 19 (4), 453–75.

Prynne, M. (2014) 'Ofsted chief "spitting blood" over right-wing attacks', *The Daily Telegraph*, 26 January. Online. www.telegraph.co.uk/education/10597751/Ofsted-chief-spitting-blood-over-right-wing-attacks.html (accessed 13 April 2014).

Putnam, R.D. (2001) *Bowling Alone: The collapse and revival of American community*. New York: Simon and Schuster.

Puttick, R. (ed.) (2011) *Using Evidence to Improve Social Policy and Practice: Perspectives on how research and evidence can influence decision making*. London: NESTA. Online. www.nesta.org.uk/sites/default/files/using_evidence_to_improve_social_policy_and_practice.pdf (accessed 15 May 2015).

PWC [PricewaterhouseCoopers] (2008) *Academies Evaluation: Fifth annual report*. London: Department for Education and Skills.

Ravitch, D. (2010) 'The myth of charter schools'. *The New York Times*, 11 November. Online. www.nybooks.com/articles/archives/2010/nov/11/myth-charter-schools/ (accessed 15 November 2010).

RCUK [Research Councils UK] (2015) 'RCUK reaffirms its commitment to Pathways to Impact following review'. Online. www.rcuk.ac.uk/media/announcements/150115/ (accessed 4 October 2015).

Reay, D. (2004) 'Education and cultural capital: The implications of changing trends in education policies'. *Cultural Trends*, 13 (2), 73–86.

— (2008) 'Tony Blair, the promotion of the "active" educational citizen, and middle-class hegemony'. *Oxford Review of Education*, 34, 639–50.

Reay, D., Crozier, G. and Clayton, J. (2009) 'Strangers in paradise? Working-class students in elite universities'. *Sociology*, 43 (6), 1,103–31.

Reay, D., Crozier, G. and James, D. (2013) *White Middle-Class Identities and Urban Schooling*. Basingstoke: Palgrave Macmillan.

Reay, D., David, M. and Ball, S.J. (2005) *Degrees of Choice: Social class, race and gender in higher education*. Stoke-on-Trent: Trentham Books.

Relay GSE [Graduate School of Education] (2013) 'Our history'. Online. http://web.archive.org/web/20141203171547/www.relay.edu/history (accessed 12 December 2014).

Reynolds, J.R. and Baird, C.L. (2010) 'Is there a downside to shooting for the stars? Unrealized education expectations and symptoms of depression'. *American Sociological Review*, 75 (1), 151–72.

Riddell, R. (2010) *Aspiration, Identity and Self-belief: Snapshots of social structure at work*. Stoke-on-Trent: Trentham Books.

Ringrose, J. (2013) *Postfeminist Education? Girls and the sexual politics of schooling*. London: Routledge.

Robbins, L. (1963) 'Higher education: Report and appendices'. CMND 2154. London: HMSO.

Roberts, N. and Foster, D. (2015) 'Initial teacher training in England'. Briefing Paper No. 6710, 7 July. London: House of Commons Library.

Rudduck, J. (1994) 'Enlarging the democratic promise of education'. Presidential address to the British Educational Research Association, University of Oxford, September.

Rudduck, J. and McIntyre, D. (eds) (1998) *Challenges for Educational Research*. London: Paul Chapman.

Sabatier, P.A. and Jenkins-Smith, H. (eds) (1993) *Policy Change and Learning: An advocacy coalition approach*. Boulder, CO: Westview Press.

Sabatier, P.A. and Weible, C.M. (2007) 'The Advocacy Coalition Framework. Innovations and clarifications'. In Sabatier, P.A. (ed.), *Theories of the Policy Process*. Boulder, CO: Westview Press.

Sahlberg, P. (2011) *Finnish Lessons: What can the world learn from educational change in Finland?* New York, NY: Teachers College Press.

— (2012) 'How GERM is infecting schools around the world'. *The Washington Post*, 29 June. Online. www.washingtonpost.com/blogs/answer-sheet/post/how-germ-is-infecting-schools-around-the-world/2012/06/29/gJQAVELZAW_blog.html (accessed 25 August 2015).

— (2015) 'Manifestations of the Global Educational Reform Movement'. In Jokila, S., Kallo, J. and Rinne, R. (eds), *Comparing Times and Spaces*. Jvaskyla, Finland: Finnish Educational Research Association.

Schriewer, J. (1990) 'The method of comparison and the need for externalization: Methodological criteria and sociological concepts'. In Schriewer, J. in cooperation with Holmes, B. (eds), *Theories and Methods in Comparative Education*. Frankfurt am Main, Bern, New York and Paris: Peter Lang.

Schuller, T., Preston, J., Hammond, C., Brassett-Grundy, A. and Bynner, J. (2004) *The Benefits of Learning: The impact of education on health, family life and social capital*. London: Routledge.

Scott, P. (1995) *The Meanings of Mass Higher Education*. Buckingham: Open University Press.

Scott, S. (2015) 'Teacher training changes will pit providers against each other'. *Schools Week*, 23 June. http://schoolsweek.co.uk/nctl-registration-changes-pit-teacher-training-providers-against-each-other/ (accessed 28 June 2015).

Sellgren, K. (2015) 'A-levels and GCSEs: Traditional exam subjects making comeback'. Online. www.bbc.com/news/education-33787751 (accessed 25 August 2015).

Sharp, R. and Green, A. (1975) *Education and Social Control: A study in progressive primary education*. London: Routledge & Kegan Paul.

Sharples, J. (2013) *Evidence for the Frontline*. London: Alliance for Useful Evidence. Online. www.alliance4usefulevidence.org/assets/EVIDENCE-FOR-THE-FRONTLINE-FINAL-5-June-2013.pdf (accessed 18 May 2015).

Shiner, M. and Noden, P. (2015) '"Why are you applying there?": "Race", class and the construction of higher education "choice" in the United Kingdom'. *British Journal of Sociology of Education*, 36 (8), 1,170–91.

Simon, B. (1976) 'Contemporary problems in educational theory'. *Marxism Today*, 20, 169–77.

Slater, J. (2005) 'Meshed in web of power'. *Times Educational Supplement*, 22 July.

Social Mobility Child Poverty Commission [SMCPC] (2013) *Higher Education: The fair access challenge*. London: SMCPC.

Smithers, A. and Robinson, P. (2011) *The Good Teacher Training Guide 2011*. Buckingham: University of Buckingham.

Southgate, E. and Bennett, A. (2014) 'Excavating widening participation policy in Australian higher education: Subject positions, representational effects, emotion'. *Creative Approaches to Research*, 7 (1), 21–45.

Stake, R. (1995) *The Art of Case Study Research*. London: Sage.

Starks, L. (2011) *The National Strategies: Evaluation of the support and resources for narrowing the gap*. Leeds: York Consulting LLP.

Stearns, K. (1996) *School Reform: Lessons from England*. Princeton: Carnegie Foundation for the Advancement of Teaching.

Steiner-Khamsi, G. and Quist, H. (2000) 'The politics of educational borrowing: Reopening the case of Achimota in British Ghana'. *Comparative Education Review*, 44 (3), 272–99.

References

Steiner-Khamsi, G., Silova, I. and Johnson, E.M. (2006) 'Neoliberalism liberally applied: Educational policy borrowing in Central Asia'. In Ozga, J., Seddon, T. and Popkewitz, T.S. (eds), *World Yearbook of Education 2006*. Abingdon and New York: Routledge.

Stewart, W. (2011) 'The challenge now is to hang on to this success'. *Times Educational Supplement*, 25 March. Online. www.tes.co.uk/article.aspx?storycode=6074357 (accessed 25 August 2015).

Sutton Trust, The (2008) 'University admissions by individual schools'. London: The Sutton Trust.

— (2012) 'The use of the pupil premium: NFER Teacher Voice Omnibus 2012 survey'. Slough: National Foundation for Educational Research.

— (2014) 'Access gap at top unis is still ten-fold, as poll shows support for lower fees for students from lower income families'. Press release, 13 August. London: The Sutton Trust.

Sylva, K. (2004) 'Briefing note from Effective Provision of Pre-school Education (EPPE)'. Project for ESRC/OUDES Working Day on Applied and Practice Based Research, 16 July.

Takayama, K. and Apple, M.W. (2008) 'The cultural politics of borrowing: Japan, Britain, and the narrative of educational crisis'. *British Journal of Sociology of Education*, 29 (3), 289–301.

Taylor, C. (2013) 'Towards a school-led education system'. Speech to the North of England Education Conference, 18 January. Online. www.gov.uk/government/speeches/charlie-taylors-keynote-speech-to-the-north-of-england-education-conference (accessed 24 November 2013).

Tooley, J. and Darby, D. (1998) *Educational Research: A critique*. London: Office for Standards in Education.

Torres, C.A. (ed.) (1998) *Education, Power and Personal Biography: Dialogues with critical educators*. London: Routledge.

Tough, S., Sasia, A. and Whitty, G. (2008) *Productive Partnerships? An examination of schools' links with higher education*. London: The Sutton Trust.

Trow, M. (1974) 'Problems in the transition from elite to mass higher education'. In OECD (ed.), *Policies for Higher Education*. General Report on the Conference on Future Structures of Post-Secondary Education held in Paris, 26–9 June 1973. Paris: OECD.

Turner, J. (2015) 'Weighing up the evidence'. Online. www.suttontrust.com/newsarchive/weighing-up-the-evidence/ (accessed 10 June 2015).

Tymms, P. (2004) 'Are standards rising in English primary schools?' *British Educational Research Journal*, 30 (4), 477–94.

Tymms, P., Coe, R. and Merrell, C. (2005) 'Standards in English schools: Changes since 1997 and the impact of government policies and initiatives. A report for the Sunday Times'. Durham: CEM Centre, University of Durham.

Tymms, P. and Merrell, C. (2007) 'Standards and quality in English primary schools over time: The national evidence. Primary Review interim report, research survey 4/1'. Cambridge: The Primary Review.

Universities and College Admissions Service [UCAS] (2012) 'How have applications for full-time undergraduate higher education in the UK changed in 2012?' Cheltenham: UCAS.

— (2014) 'End of cycle report 2014'. UCAS 102811. Cheltenham: UCAS.

Universities' Council for the Education of Teachers [UCET] (2013) 'UCET objects to Ofsted press release'. Letter dated 25 March. Online. www.ucet.ac.uk/downloads/4745-25-March-2013-UCET-objects-to-OFSTED-press-release.pdf (accessed 1 October 2015).

UK Statistics Authority. Letter from Sir Andrew Dilnot, chair of the UK Statistics Authority, to David Miliband MP. 3 October 2012. Online. www.statisticsauthority.gov.uk/reports—correspondence/correspondence/letter-from-andrew-dilnot-to-rt–hon–david-miliband-mp—03102012.pdf (accessed 1 October 2015).

US Department of Education (1986) *What Works: Research about teaching and learning.* Washington, DC: US Department of Education.

Urban Teacher Residency United [UTRU] (2015) *Clinically Oriented Teacher Preparation.* Chicago, IL: UTRU.

Universities United Kingdom [UUK] (2013) *The Power of Part-Time: Review of part-time and mature higher education.* London: Universities UK.

Van Dyke, R., Little, B. and Callender, C. (2005) *Survey of Higher Education Students' Attitudes to Debt and Term-Time Working and their Impact on Attainment.* Bristol: HEFCE.

Vasagar, J. (2010) 'Free meals scrapped to pay for school improvement scheme'. Online. www.guardian.co.uk/politics/2010/nov/02/free-meals-school-improvement-scheme (accessed 15 November 2010).

Vignoles, A. and Crawford, C. (2010) 'Access, participation and diversity questions in relation to different forms of post-compulsory further and higher education (FHEs)'. In David, M. (ed.), *Improving Learning by Widening Participation in Higher Education.* Abingdon: Routledge.

Vignoles, A. and Powdthavee, N. (2009) 'The socioeconomic gap in university dropouts'. *The B. E. Journal of Economic Analysis*, 9 (1), 19–39.

Ward, H. (2015) 'Why schools must "wake up" to the reality of racist bullying'. *Times Educational Supplement*, No. 5164, 18 September, 10.

Warry, P. (2006) *Increasing the Economic Impact of the Research Councils: Advice to the Director General of Science and Innovation, DTI from the Research Council Economic Impact Group.* RCUK Report No. 06/1678. Swindon: RCUK.

Weber, K. (ed.) (2010) *Waiting for 'Superman': How we can save America's failing public schools.* New York, NY: Public Affairs.

Weiss, C.H. (1991) 'Policy research: Data, ideas or arguments?'. In Wagner, P., Weiss, C., Wittrock, B. and Wollmann, H. (eds), *Social Sciences and Modern States: National experiences and theoretical crossroads.* Cambridge: Cambridge University Press.

What Works Network (2014) *What Works? Evidence for decision-makers.* London: Cabinet Office. Online. www.gov.uk/government/publications/what-works-evidence-for-decision-makers (accessed 16 April 2015).

Whiting, C., Whitty, G., Furlong, J., Miles, S. and Barton, L. (1996) *Partnership in Initial Teacher Education: A topography.* London: Institute of Education.

Whitty, G. (1974) 'Sociology and the problem of radical educational change'. In Flude, M. and Ahier, J. (eds), *Educability, Schools and Ideology.* London: Croom Helm.

— (1985) *Sociology and School Knowledge: Curriculum, theory, research and politics.* London: Methuen.

— (1989) 'The New Right and the national curriculum: State control or market forces?' *Journal of Education Policy*, 4 (4), 329–41.

— (1991) *Next in Line for the Treatment? Education reform and teacher education in the 1990s.* London: Goldsmiths College.

— (1997) *Social Theory and Education Policy: The legacy of Karl Mannheim.* London: Institute of Education.

— (2000) 'Teacher professionalism in new times'. *Journal of In-Service Education*, 26 (2), 281–95.

— (2001) 'Education, social class and social exclusion', *Journal of Education Policy*, 16 (4), 287–95.

— (2002) *Making Sense of Education Policy: Studies in the sociology and politics of education.* London: Sage.

References

— (2004) 'Developing comprehensive education in a new climate'. In Benn, M. and Chitty, C. (eds), *A Tribute to Caroline Benn*. London: Continuum.
— (2006) 'Education(al) research and education policy making: Is conflict inevitable?' *British Educational Research Journal*, 32 (2), 159–76.
— (2008) 'Twenty years of progress? English education policy 1988 to the present'. *Educational Management Administration & Leadership*, 36 (2), 165–84.
— (2009) 'Evaluating "Blair's educational legacy"? Some comments on the special issue of *Oxford Review of Education*'. *Oxford Review of Education*, 35, 267–80.
— (2010a) 'Revisiting school knowledge: Some sociological perspectives on new school curricula'. *European Journal of Education*, 45, 28–45.
— (2010b) 'A decade of achievement: Interview with Diane Hofkins'. *Alumni Life* (IOE), winter, 9–10.
— (2013) 'Educational research and teacher education in higher education institutions in England'. Paper presented at the State of the Nations Panel, HEA Summit, Milton Keynes, 17 January. Online. www.heacademy.ac.uk/sites/default/files/resources/learningtoteach_part1_final.pdf (accessed 1 October 2015).
— (2014) 'Recent developments in teacher training and their consequences for the "University Project" in education'. *Oxford Review of Education*, 40 (4), 466–81.
Whitty, G. and Clement, N. (2015) 'Getting into Uni in England and Australia: Who you know, what you know or knowing the ropes?' *International Studies in Widening Participation*, 2 (2) (forthcoming).
Whitty, G. and Edwards, T. (1998) 'School choice policies in England and the United States: An exploration of their origins and significance'. *Comparative Education*, 34 (2), 211–27.
Whitty, G. and Mullan, J. (2013) 'Postgraduate education: Overlooked and forgotten?' In Callender, C. and Scott, P. (eds), *Browne and Beyond: Modernizing English higher education*. London: IOE Press.
Whitty, G., Power, S. and Halpin, D. (1998) *Devolution and Choice in Education: The school, the state and the market*. Buckingham: Open University Press.
Whitty, G. and Young, M. (eds) (1976) *Explorations in the Politics of School Knowledge*. Driffield: Studies in Education Ltd.
Wiliam, D. (2015) 'The research delusion'. *Times Educational Supplement*, 10 April.
Wilkes, G. (2014) *The Unelected Lynchpin: Why government needs special advisers*. Online. www.instituteforgovernment.org.uk/sites/default/files/publications/InsideOut%20SPAD%20The%20Unelected%20Lynchpin_0.pdf (accessed 7 May 2015).
Wilkins, A. and Burke, P.J. (2015) 'Widening participation in higher education: The role of professional and social class identities and commitments'. *British Journal of Sociology of Education*, 36 (3), 434–52.
Willis, P. (1977) *Learning to Labour: How working class kids get working class jobs*. Farnborough: Saxon House.
Witte, J. (1993) 'The Milwaukee Parental Choice Program: The first thirty months'. Paper delivered at the Annual Meeting of the American Educational Research Association, Atlanta, Georgia.
Wolf, A. (2011) *Review of Vocational Education (The Wolf Report)*. London: Department for Education.
Wolf, R. (2010) 'New schools and real parental choice'. *The Guardian*, 20 February. Online. www.guardian.co.uk/commentisfree/2010/feb/20/education-choice-new-schools (accessed 15 November 2010).
Wyness, G. (2011) *London Schooling: Lessons from the capital*. London: CentreForum.
Wyse, D. and Parker, C. (2012) *The Early Literacy Handbook*. London: MA Education Ltd.

Yan, F. and Whitty, G. (in press) 'Towards inter-cultural education in Xinjiang, North-west China?' In Bash, L. and Coulby, D. (eds), *Establishing a Culture of Intercultural Education.* Cambridge: Cambridge Scholars Publishing.

Yates, L. (2005) 'Is impact a measure of quality? Producing quality research and producing quality indicators of research in Australia'. Keynote address to the Australian Association for Research in Education Focus Conference on 'Quality in Educational Research: Directions in policy and practice', Cairns, July.

Young, M. (ed.) (1971) *Knowledge and Control: New directions for the sociology of education.* London: Collier–MacMillan.

— (2008a) *Bringing Knowledge Back In: From social constructivism to social realism in the sociology of education.* London: Routledge.

— (2008b) 'Shopping for skills'. *RSA Journal,* 154, 30–3.

— (2009) 'What are schools for?' In Daniels, H., Lauder, H. and Porter, J. (eds), *Knowledge, Values and Educational Policy: A critical perspective.* London: Routledge.

— (2010) 'Alternative educational futures for a knowledge society'. *European Educational Research Journal,* 9 (1), 1–12.

— (2011) 'The return to subjects: A sociological perspective on the UK Coalition Government's approach to the 14–19 curriculum'. *Curriculum Journal,* 22 (2), 265–78.

Young, M. and Whitty, G. (eds) (1977) *Society, State and Schooling: Readings on the possibilities for radical education.* Lewes: Falmer Press.

Zimdars, A., Sullivan, A. and Heath, A. (2009) 'Elite higher education admissions in the arts and sciences: Is cultural capital the key?' *Sociology,* 43 (4), 648–66.

Index

academic capital 83
academy schools 12–13, 29, 42, 46–7, 59, 62–70, 103
achievement gap 55–73, 94, 103, 107–8; factors in narrowing of 59–72; trends in 56–9
Advanced Level (A-level) exams 80
advocacy organizations 11, 15, 46–7
Aimhigher initiative 46, 75, 79–82, 85
Allen, G. 72
Alliance for Useful Evidence 8
Anders, J. ix, 88, 94 (co-author)
anecdotal evidence 47–8
Anglia Ruskin University 33
apprenticeships 80
Archer, L. 92
ARK chain of schools 28
aspirations of school pupils 85–6, 92–4
assisted places scheme 43–4
Association of School and College Leaders (ASCL) 23
Atherton, G. 85
attainment gap *see* achievement gap
Australia 4

Baars, S. 67
Ball, S.J. 5–6, 17, 29, 44, 70, 90, 100, 102
Banks, O. 99–100, 107
Barber, M. 26–7, 64
Bastedo, M. 76
Bath Spa University 34–5
Bathmaker, A.-M. 93
Beck, J. 106
Bell, D. 29
Bennett, T. 2
Bernstein, B. 68, 86, 97–100, 104–6
Big Lottery Fund 8
Birmingham University 34
Blair, Tony 4, 26–7, 50, 56, 68, 75, 103
Bloomberg, M. 41
Blueprint for Reform reports 50–1
Blunkett, D. 5, 11, 18
Bok, J. 86
Boliver, V. 77, 88
Bourdieu, P. 83, 88–9, 102
Bowles, S. 101
Boyer, E.L. 39–40
Bradley Foundation 47
breadth of research base 18
Brighouse, T. 65, 68
Bristol Polytechnic 102
British Educational Research Association (BERA) 10, 36
Brookings Institution 40
Brown, C. 16
Browne Report (2010) 79, 85
Burgess, S. 67
Burke, P.J. 83, 91–2, 94
bursaries for students 84–5

Callender, C. 81, 83–6
Cambridge University 78
Campaign for Social Science 10
Canada, G. 41–2
careers education 86
Carter, A. 24
Centre for Policy Studies 47
'chains' of schools 68–9
charter schools 28, 40–2, 46–50, 53
Chartered London Teacher scheme 66
Children's Plan (2007) 62
China 36, 45, 47
Chira, S. 47
Chowdry, H. 78
Christie, C. 41
Christodoulou, D. 98, 103
Chubb, J. 38, 40, 47
City Challenge scheme 66, 69
city technology colleges 44
Clarke, C. 5, 18
Clarke, F. 107
class size 11–12
'clinical practice' models of teacher preparation 36
Coalition Government (2010–2015), policies of 6–8, 11–14, 24–9, 32, 43, 50, 58–9, 63, 68–73, 79–82, 85, 103
Collins, K. 2
communities of practice 52
'compensatory education' 105
comprehensive education 99
Connexions 80
Conservative policies 31, 43, 68, 70, 80–2, 102–3
consultancies 16–17
'contingent choosers' 90–1
Cook, C. 57
Corbyn, J. 94
Core Knowledge Foundation 103
Corrigan, P. 101
Council for the Accreditation of Teacher Education (CATE) 20, 26
Coyne, J. 92
Crawford, C. 78, 88
CREDO study 49–50
critical research 18
cultural capital 83, 88–93, 108
curriculum policy 69–70
Curtis, A. 63, 69, 92

Davies, P. 84, 89–91
Dawson, G. 101
Dearden, L. 85
debt aversion 84
Deloitte (firm) 28
Demack, S. 91
Department for Business, Innovation and Skills (BIS) 81, 91
Department for Education (DfE) 3, 6, 48–9, 81
devolution of decision-making 6
Diversity in Teacher Education (DiTE), research on 34–6

Index

dominant discourses of educational reform 46–50
dropout from higher education 85, 93
Duncan, A. 42

Earl, L. 60–1
early years provision 14
Ebdon, L. 79
Economic and Social Research Council (ESRC) 3, 7–9
education action zones 56, 59–60
Education Endowment Foundation (EEF) 6–7, 10, 71
Education Endowment Fund 42–3
Education Media Centre 8
education policy-making, empirical studies of 101
Education Reform Act (1988) 25
education research: criticisms of 9–10, 28; scope of 1; in tension with policy and practice 18; under successive governments 3–9
'education science' model of research 9, 18
educational sociology 99; *see also* sociology of education
Edwards, A.D.; also referred to as Edwards, T. 44, 53, 101–2
Effective Provision of Pre-school Education (EPPE/EPPSE) project 14–15
'effectively managed inequality' (EMI) 76
'elite measures' 72
embedding of knowledge exchange 7
employment prospects of former students 93–4
English Baccalaureate 70, 103
ethnic minority groups 55
ethnographic studies 101
Every Child a Reader programme 64
Every Child Matters agenda 46, 59
evidence-informed policy 2–8, 11–18, 20, 32, 46, 59–60
Evidence for Policy and Practice Information and Coordinating Centre (EPPI Centre) 4
Excellence in Cities programme 59–60
exclusionary practices in higher education 91–2
Exley, S. 70
expenditure on research 4, 6
experimental research 3
'extended' schools 63–4
Eyles, A. 63

Fabian Society 53, 98–9
'fact-checking' movement 9
'fair access' principle 75, 79–88, 93; *see also* Office for Fair Access
family background of students 92
Fantini, M. 106
Feinberg, M. 43
Field, F. 72
Finland 24, 36, 45–6
'floor targets' 59
Floud, J. 99–100
formative assessment 14

free school meals, recipients of 55, 57, 61, 64–70, 87, 90
'free schools' 29, 42–3, 46–9, 68, 103
Friedman, S. 94
'full-service' schools 63
Furlong, J. 4, 27

Gale, T. 94–5
gender differences in educational achievement 55, 61
General Certificate of Secondary Education (GCSE) 57, 80
General Teaching Council 25
Gewirtz, S. 5, 17
Gibb, N. 24, 31
Gilbert, C. 21
Gillborn, D. 72
Gintis, H. 101
Glass, G. 50–1
globalization 38–9, 50, 52, 54
Goldacre, B. 6–7
Goldstein, H. 12, 60–1
Goodfellow, J.M. 92
Gorard, S. 12–13, 82
Gove, M. 13, 22, 24, 27–8, 31–2, 42–3, 48, 66–7, 70, 103, 106
graduate premium 90
Graduate Teacher Programme (GTP) 21
grammar school education 86, 97–8
Gramsci, A. 103
grant-maintained schools 40, 42, 46
Greaves, E. 67
Green, A. 101
Green, D. 40
Grek, S. 45
Griffiths, S. 48
Gulson, K. 95
Gumport, P. 76
gypsy, Roma and traveller (GRT) children 61

habitus 89, 91–2
Halsey, A.H. 100, 107
Hargreaves, A. 52
Hargreaves, D. 5, 100
Harris, M. 78, 92–3
Hayton, A. ix (co-author)
Henig, J.R. 53
Her Majesty's Inspectorate of Schools (HMI) 40
Hibernia College, Dublin 33
hierarchy of influence 16
'highbrow culture' 90
higher education: access to 56, 74–6, 82, 85, 95; funding of 4, 7–8, 79, 81, 83, 94
Hillgate Group 30
Hirsch, E.D. 103
Hirst, P. 104
Hodge, S. 95
Holmwood, J. 10, 17
House of Commons Education Committee 13, 25, 63, 69
Hudson Institute 47

Index

Husbands, C. 33–4
Hutchings, M. 66–7, 69

impact acceleration accounts (IAAs) 7
impact of research 7–8, 10, 15, 17
'impact summaries' in grant applications 7
Income Deprivation Affecting
  Children Index (IDAC) 57–8
inequalities in education 75–81, 91, 106
'informed prescription' 26
'initiative-itis' 59
Institute of Economic Affairs 40, 47
Institute of Education (IOE), London 25, 34, 64,
  86, 92, 97–100, 108
Institute of Employment Studies 84
Institute for Fiscal Studies (IFS) 81, 86
Institute for Public Policy Research 16
instrumental view of research 5
International comparisons 13, 45

Jackson, J. 83–6
Jerrim, J. 13, 61
Jin, W. 85

Keddie, N. 106
Kelly, R. 14
Kerr, K. 55, 72
'Keys to Success' schools 65–7
Klein, J. 43
Knowledge is Power Programme (KIPP) 43

Labour Party 94, 99; *see also*
  New Labour policies
Lacey, C. 100
Laurison, D. 94
Lawton, D. 16
Learning and Teaching Toolkit 6, 71
Leverhulme Trust 3
Levin, B. 51–3
Liberal Democrat Party 70, 79, 81
Literacy Strategy and the 'literacy hour' 59–62
local management of schools 44
London Challenge 59, 65–9
Lubienski, C. 49

McCaig, C. 81, 94
Machin, S. 60–3
McKinsey (consultancy) 16
MacLaury, Bruce K. 39
McManus, J. 91–2
McNally, S. 60–1
Maden, M. 62
maintenance grants for students 75, 80, 82
Manchester School of educational sociology 100
Mangan, J. 91
Manhattan Institute 47
Mann, H. 39, 52–3
Mannheim, K. 98–9
marketization 27–8
Mathis, W. 50–1
media reporting on education 47
'medical model' of education research 3

mentoring 95
Menzies, L. 85–6
Metcalfe, A. 95
middle-class children, education of
  89–92, 102, 108
Milburn Review of Access to
  the Professions (2009) 85
Miliband, D. 40
Miliband, E. 96n6
Modes of Teacher Education
  (MOTE) project 34–5
Moe, T. 39–40, 47
Moore, C. 31
Morgan, N. 24
Morris, R. 69
Mortimore, P. 72
Mourshed, M. 64
Muijs, D. 64
Mythbuster 48–50

'naïve possibilitarianism' 101
National Audit Office (NAO) 62
National College for Teaching
  and Leadership 25
National Commission on Education 53
National Coordinating Centre for
  Public Engagement (NCCPE) 7
National Curriculum 29, 32, 40, 102
National Educational Research Forum
  (NERF) 5–6
National Foundation for Educational
  Research (NFER) 86
National Network for Collaborative Outreach 82
National Scholarship Programme (NSP) 79, 81
National Strategy for Access
  and Student Success 82, 93
'navigation' of educational pathways 86
neo-conservative policies 30, 43, 70, 102–4
neo-liberal policies 30, 43–4, 102
neo-Marxist analysis 101
Nesta (charity) 8
network governance 16–17
New Labour policies 5–16, 20–1, 25–7, 43, 55–9,
  62–8, 71, 75, 78–9, 83, 103
New Right pressure groups 30–1, 44, 101
New Schools Network 47
Nisbet, J. 3, 5, 16
'No Child Left Behind' program (in the US) 46
Noble, J. 89–90
Noden, P. 89
Nuffield Foundation 47
Numeracy Strategy 59–62

Oakley, A. 6
Obama, B. 40–5, 50
Ochs, K. 38, 44, 46
Office for Fair Access (OFFA) 75, 78–9
Office for Standards in Education (Ofsted)
  3, 13, 21–2, 26–7, 32, 61, 65–71, 80
O'Hear, A. 31
Ontario Institute for Studies in Education
  (OISE) 47
Open University 33, 101

133

Index

Organization for Economic Co-operation and Development (OECD)   36, 45
Osborne, G.   81
outreach activities of universities   75, 79–82, 92, 95
'over-aspiring' students   92
Overseas Trained Teacher Programme (OTTP)   21
Oxford University   28, 77–8, 91

parental education   90
'participation gap' in higher education   74–8, 87–8
peer tutoring   71
performance indicators for schools   81
Phillips, D.   38, 44, 46
policy and practice, research-informed   1–16
policy borrowing, transatlantic   38–54
policy convergence   43–4
'policy epidemics'   52
Policy Exchange   69
Policy Forum   67
'policy tourism'   38–41, 47, 52
'political arithmetic' tradition   98–9, 102, 107
Pollard, A.   9, 15
Postgraduate Certificate in Education (PGCE)   24, 26
postmodernism   102, 106
'poverty of aspiration' thesis   85
Powdthavee, N.   93
'powerful knowledge'   70, 104
PriceWaterhouseCoopers   12, 62
'prior attainment' of students   56, 86–8
private schooling   77–8, 101–2
professionalism of teachers   26–9, 35
Programme for International Student Assessment (PISA)   45
'progression' measures   71
'progressive' approaches to education   103
'public intellectuals'   17, 53
public opinion   17, 53
pupil premium   70–1

'qualified teacher' status (QTS)   20–1, 24, 26, 29, 35
'qualitative inequalities' in education   78, 81, 91
qualitative and quantitative research   6
'quantitative inequalities' in education   75–81, 91
quasi-experimental methods of research   64
quasi-research   46

Race to the Top   43, 46, 50
randomized control trials (RCTs)   3, 6, 16
Ravitch, D.   41, 50, 67–8, 72–3
Reading Recovery programme   14, 59, 64
Reay, D.   89
redistributive policies   94
Reform (pressure group)   17
Relay Graduate School of Education   28
Research Assessment Exercise (RAE)   8–9
Research Councils UK   7
Research Excellence Framework (REF)   8–10, 15, 17

research literacy   36
'research for use'   1–2, 8, 15–17
Researchers in Schools scheme   24
Robbins Report (1963)   74
Robinson, P.   21
Romer, R.   41
Royal Society of Arts   36
Rudduck, J.   3
Russell Group universities   77–8, 91

Sabatier, P.   44
Sahlberg, P.   38, 53
School Direct scheme   22–3, 32–3
school examinations   80
school performance tables   70
school–university links   80, 92, 94–5
Schools Research Liaison Group   5
Schools Week   33
Schriewer, J.   44–5
'science capital' concept   92
Scott, P.   81
Secondary National Strategy   14
See, B.H.   82
selective use of research findings   48–51
Sharp, R.   101
Shiner, M.   89
Simon, B.   104
Singapore   27
Smithers, A.   21
social capital   83, 88, 93–4
social justice   55, 70, 94–5
Social Mobility and Child Poverty Commission   78
Social Mobility Strategy   59
social science   10, 17
socio-economic status, impact of differences in   55–8, 62–3, 76–8, 84–90, 93, 95
sociology of education   97–108; concern with socal inequalities   107; and education policy   101–2, 106–8; 'old' and 'new'   98–104; political influence of   107
specialist schools   12–13, 59
Spencer Foundation   47
Stake, R.   38
stakeholders in education   15–16
Stearns, K.   39–40
Steiner-Khamsi, G.   38, 44–6
Stewart, W.A.C.   99
Stuart, G.   32–3
student finance   79, 82–5
summative assessment   14
Sutton Trust   78, 89, 91–2
Sweden   48
Sylva, K.   15
synthetic phonics   69
systematic reviews   3–4, 6

Tang, S.   ix (co-author)
targeted interventions   14
Taylor, C.   29–30
Teach First scheme   21, 23, 28, 31–2, 40–1, 64–6
Teach for America scheme   40, 64

Index

teacher education and training 2, 20–36; changes in policy for 26–9; deregulation of 29, 32; diversity in 34–6; employment-based 21; future prospects for 29–34; by partnerships between schools and higher-education institutions 20–8, 31–4; reforms by Coalition and Conservative governments 21–5; school-centred schemes (SCITTs) 20–5, 31–4; small systems for 29–30
Teacher Training Agency (TTA) 3, 20, 25–6
teacher training schools 22, 27
teaching assistants 17, 59–60
Technology Colleges Trust 12
Thatcher, M. 3, 20, 26, 30, 40, 68, 102
think tanks 16–17, 46–7, 53
Times Educational Supplement 16, 32
Training and Development Agency for Schools (TDA) 25–6
transposability of education policies 52
trials-led research 6
Troops to Teachers scheme 23
tuition fees 75, 85
Turner, J. 18
Tymms, P. 13, 60

United Kingdom Statistics Authority 13
United States 4, 9, 28, 64, 73; *see also* policy borrowing: transatlantic
Universities' Council for the Education of Teachers (UCET) 32
University of Bath 26, 33, 100
university training schools 24

value added models (VAM) 35
Vernoit, J. 62
Vignoles, A. 93

Walker, S. 28–9
Warwick University 33, 40
Weinstein, G. 106
Welner, K. 50–1
West, M. 55, 72
'what doesn't work' 52–3
'what works' approach to education research 1, 3–4, 9–10, 38, 46, 50–4, 59–60, 71
'what works centres' 7
Whitty, G. ix, 27, 30–3, 44, 53, 72, 97–105, 108 (principal author)
widening participation in higher education 56, 75–88, 93–5; barriers to 82–8
Wiliam, D. 2
Willis, P. 101
Wilshaw, M. 22, 32
Wisby, E. x (co-author)
Wolf, R. 47–8
Wolf Report (2011) 80
working-class children, education of 100–7
world-class education 45
Wyness, G. 65

York Consulting 61
Young, M. 98–105

Zimdars, A. 91